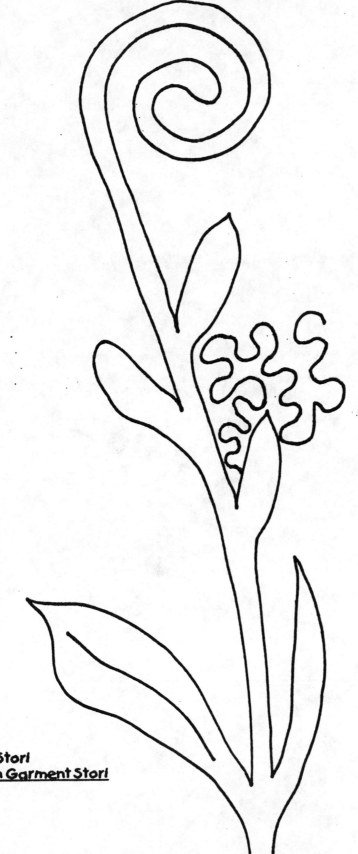

1998 Mary Stori
Wholecloth Garment Stori

THE STORI OF WHOLE-CLOTH GARMENTS

Select a simple pattern that has some shape but no darts.

Trace pattern pieces <u>one size</u> larger than your finished size to a large sheet of paper. If minimum quilting is planned, trace your correct size.

Trace your correct size pattern onto see-through tracing material to use later.

Using stencils or freezer paper cutouts of your design subject - play on the paper patterns until you find a pleasing arrangement. Don't put important design elements in the seam allowance. Document final design by retracing with a black permanent pen. The more design elements you have, the less background quilting you'll have to do..... a consideration if stippling!

Cut one piece each (for every paper pattern piece you've designed): fashion fabric, batting, and muslin (underlining) backing. Rectangular pieces usually work best for garment fronts and a square for one-piece backs....allow a margin of at least 4" larger than the garment shape.

Before basting the fabrics together......trace the design onto the right side of your fashion fabric. A lightbox or window can be helpful here. TEST YOUR MARKING TOOLS BEFORE BEGINNING!!!

NOTE - designs created using stencils can be retraced onto the fashion fabric using the original stencil. Even if you've done some minor adjusting and adapting......as long as you refer to your original drawing it should be ok.

To <u>Thread</u> baste: (a.) I tape my precut bottom layer (muslin backing) to my cutting table. (b.) cover with the precut batting piece (c.) top with the marked fashion fabric (d.) thread baste as usual. **Note:** it's also helpful to baste the shape of the garment piece, using a smaller stitch length. If your marking lines rub off, this will provide a guide to let you know where to stop the background stipple quilting.

Begin quilting....always outline quilt your design first.....then stipple quilt the background if desired.

The trapunto/stuffing/cording is (almost always) done last. Always remove fabric from hoop or frame for this process. <u>Overfilling will cause distortion!!!</u>

If the edges have rippled when the section is completed (esp. when stipple quilting) - lay it **wrong side up,** flat on a table protected with towels. Use a warm iron and lightly steam the edges flat. Be <u>very</u> careful not to melt poly batting. Let cool in place before moving.

Lay your prepared **correct size see through** pattern pieces on the completed sections to reconfirm the exact shape and design placement and retrace shape. Optional - before cutting out you may wish to machine stay-stitch just outside the sewing line, in the seam allowance, to secure your hand quilting stitches. Cut out.

Sew together following pattern directions. Quilt any unquilted areas. Grade bulky seams and press. Line garment.

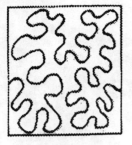

figure 1

continuous line
resembles jigsaw
puzzle pieces

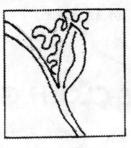

figure 2

begin in a tight area
& work out to open
spaces

figure 3

NO!! - avoid
perpendicular stitching

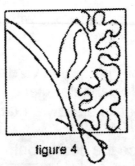

figure 4

DO NOT travel between areas to
be stuffed or trapuntoed

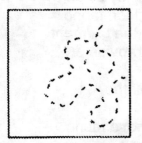

figure 5

create gentle curves by
stitching 2 stitches at a
time

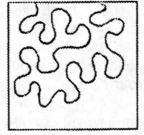

figure 6

change direction of
line often

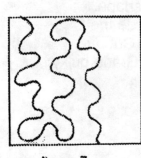

figure 7

avoid stitching in rows

Kentucky Heritage Quilt Society

P.O. Box 23392, Lexington, Ky. 40523

STOP & SMELL the ROSES
1999 KHQS Challenge Quilts

Given the rapid pace most of us live at these days, its important to remember to take time to relish some of the simple joys in life like smelling the roses.

Rules:

1. The quilt must be based on a design that dipicts or symbolizes a rose. Traditional pieced and applique blocks as well as original designs can be used as long as the re is a clearly defined rose in the design or rose is in the pattern name such as "Rose of Sharon" a traditional applique pattern or "Rose Garden" a Nancy Cabot pattern. Rose printed fabrics can be used in the pieced or applique design and cut out roses can be used to Broiderie Perse a design. The techniques used can be hand and/or machine. Don't forget three dimensional techniques like ruching.

2. The quilt must be composed of three layers--top, batting and back.

3. Use of 100% cotton is not required, but is highly advisable as the quilts will travel for a year and need to be able to stand the strain of being folded, stacked, shipped and displayed for a year.

4. The quilt may be hand or machine quilted.

5. MINIMUM SIZE : The perimeter of the quilt is to be no less than 100 inches (i.e. 25"x25").

6. MAXIMUM SIZE: The perimeter of the quilt is to be no greater than 200 inches (i.e. 50"x 50", 40" x 60 ",etc.)

7. A four-inch sleeve must be attached to the back.

8. A fabric label must be sewn to the back with your name, title of the quilt and date made.

9. The quilt must have been finished since 1997.

10. The quilt must be allowed to travel from June 1999 to June 2000.

11. The quilt must be received by May 15, 1999.

12. Mail/ship to: Karen M. Templeton, President-Elect
~~18 Sunny View Ln.~~
~~Carthage, TN. 37030~~

new address

6 - 98
FOR- Mary
Enjoy the whole
Stori !

The Wholecloth Garment Stori

Hugs,
Mary Stori

Mary Stori

American Quilter's Society
P. O. Box 3290 • Paducah, KY 42002-3290

Located in Paducah, Kentucky, the American Quilter's Society (AQS), is dedicated to promoting the accomplishments of today's quilters. Through its publications and events, AQS strives to honor today's quiltmakers and their work — and inspire future creativity and innovation in quiltmaking.

EDITOR: BARBARA SMITH
BOOK DESIGN: ANGELA SCHADE
ILLUSTRATIONS: LANETTE BALLARD, JUSTIN GREEN, AND ANGELA SCHADE
COVER DESIGN: ELAINE WILSON AND ANGELA SCHADE
PHOTOGRAPHY: CHARLES R. LYNCH, UNLESS INDICATED OTHERWISE

Library of Congress Cataloging-in-Publication Data
Stori, Mary
    The wholecloth garment stori / Mary Stori
                  p.   cm.
    ISBN 1-57342-718-6
      1. Quilting.   2. Clothing.   3. Patterns.   4. Decorative embellishments.
                          I. Title.

                              Applied for.
                              CIP

Additional copies of this book may be ordered from: American Quilter's Society, PO Box 3290, Paducah, KY 42002-3290 @ $19.95. Add $2.00 for postage & handling.

Printed in the U.S.A. by Image Graphics, Paducah, KY

Dedication

To my guys, David and Chris, for keeping my feet on the ground.

Acknowledgments

Words alone, of course, are never enough, but thank you, Betty Micheels, for all your encouragement and for putting that first needle in my hand. And thank you, Dorothy Theobald, for your ingenuity, which always set a good example.

The editor is so vital to an author, and I am indebted to Terri Nyman and Barbara Smith for their expertise. I am grateful to all the folks at the American Quilter's Society, and especially Meredith and Bill Schroeder, for their continued support of quilters everywhere.

A special thank you goes to my two dear friends—Alex Dupré for her superb machine stipple quilting on the jumper Pretty & Pink, and Sharee Dawn Roberts for enlightening me about the world of threads.

My appreciation is also extended to Pfaff American Sales Corporation and Hobbs Bonded Fibers for their generosity.

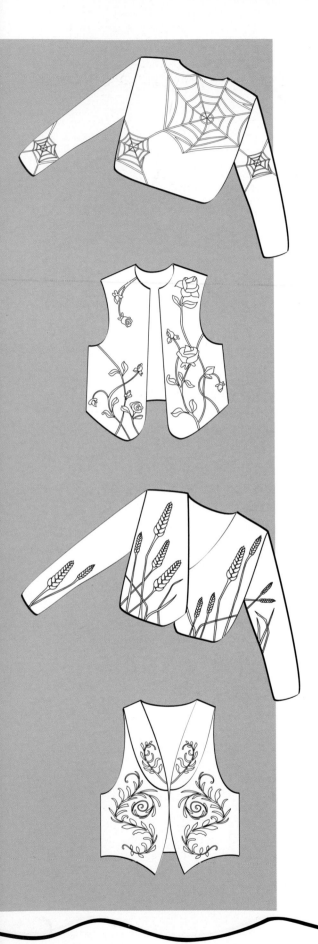

Contents

Contents

Introduction

Little did I know, when I picked up that first needle in the mid 1980s, that the world of fiber arts would become my profession. You might call me an enthusiastic late bloomer. I had no formal art training, which proved to be an advantage, because without restraints, my path was less cluttered with "do's" and "don'ts." The obstacles challenged me to find simpler ways to achieve my ideas. It is clear, however, that my previous career as a cooking instructor and cookbook author has influenced my work. I now "garnish" cloth rather than food.

I am attracted to wholecloth garments because, unlike those that have to be pieced or appliquéd, they offer me the freedom to design on a "blank canvas." (I define "wholecloth garments" as wearables constructed from a single fabric for all of the major pattern pieces.) Since I don't have to spend time piecing and appliquéing, I can start on my favorite part right away—creating designs. Garment construction is generally simplified because many of the technical difficulties often associated with pieced garments, such as matching seams, are eliminated. These garments are wonderful additions to any wardrobe because they can be worn to many different kinds of functions.

Making each new garment presents an opportunity to refine my skills and challenges me to explore unfamiliar techniques. The payoff is a finished garment that frequently bears little resemblance to my original vision, yet this unpredictability and sense of surprise keep the work fun.

This workbook of wholecloth garment projects was developed for those who are frustrated by a lack of time but who still want to produce distinctive wearable pieces to showcase their skills. By minimizing the time spent designing and experimenting, this approach allows you to successfully create unique projects in less time.

Rather than attempting to provide a one-size-fits-all garment pattern, which is rarely flattering to anyone, my goal is to share imaginative designs combined with useful construction approaches. You can recreate these designs on your own garment patterns, suitable for your figure. Each chapter introduces one of three methods. You will find complete instructions covering fabric selection, design placement, stabilizing procedures, sewing tips, and machine set-up. My method of creating machine-stitched designs is efficient and enjoyable because there's no need to use a machine embroidery hoop. Equally important, the method still allows you to secure the fabric pieces in a hoop for hand quilting, hand embroidery, and beading, if you like.

All the garments featured began with a commercial pattern, and you should have no trouble locating similar, easy-to-sew patterns at your local sewing center. Some garments are embellished with stitching only, while others are highlighted with beads or hand embroidery, which requires more dedication. The designs were created to address both hand and machine stitching, and many allow the flexibility of either approach. Within each project, line drawings of various garments are offered with suggestions for additional design ideas for consideration.

Beginners can feel secure following the step-by-step directions, while advanced sewers may want to challenge their skills by expanding on the ideas offered. This book is not intended to teach you pattern drafting, tailoring, or the basics of garment construction, and a certain level of sewing experience is taken for granted. Sewing centers,

fabric stores, libraries, and perhaps your own personal sewing library are full of books with precise instructions for basic sewing techniques.

The primary aim, of course, is to present distinctive garment projects for you to create. In the process, you can expect to add new approaches and techniques to your inventory of skills and, most of all, you can enjoy making and wearing your own wholecloth garments.

How This Stori Goes

Each chapter begins with an overview of a specific technique: stuff-work, quilting or embroidery. However, some projects introduce a variation of the general process (presented in "Stori Lines"), so please read your chosen project's instructions thoroughly before beginning.

You can either hand or machine stitch. The projects can be used as given or adapted to suit your needs. For as much versatility as possible, the designs were carefully selected to let you choose a motif from one chapter and create it using a technique from another chapter. For instance, those sewers who are experienced in machine quilting might want to use an electric needle to stitch the designs in the first chapter. Furthermore, if you like the rose designs in Chapter 1 but prefer a vest rather than a jumper, you will find additional design placement ideas for other types of garments in each chapter. Once you become familiar with the techniques, you will be ready to customize your own garments. Allow your-

self the freedom to alter any of the designs provided. Please remember, this is your project. You are in charge of the needle and thread!

Your wholecloth "stori" begins with a purchased garment pattern. Select one that is flattering to your figure and comfortable to wear. The patterns you already own may be suitable for these wholecloth projects. Because you will be sewing on fabric sections, not cut-out garment shapes, it is best to avoid styles that have darts, princess seams, two-piece sleeves and side panels.

I look for patterns that have simple, yet slightly shaped pattern pieces, which are more attractive than their boxy counterparts.

Next comes the fun part, where you get to play with the designs. You can either design on paper before transferring the design to your fabric or you can design directly on fabric.

Designing on Paper

1. If possible, buy a garment pattern that has multiple sizes. Use a black fine-line permanent pen to trace all the major pattern pieces, one size larger than you normally wear (unless otherwise noted). Make the tracing on paper, such as blank newsprint or brown craft paper. A light box may make this task easier. If the pattern you have chosen is generously sized or if you plan to do only minimal stitching, you may be able to use your correct-size pattern. If your purchased pattern does not have multiple sizes, use your correct size for designing.

2. Make a second tracing of all the major garment pattern pieces in your correct size on see-through pattern-tracing material. Cut out and retain the correct-size, see-through pattern to use later as a guide for cutting out the garment.

3. Select the designs for your garment, auditioning their position on the newsprint or brown-paper pattern. You could start by deciding where a motif will be placed or where grid lines will be drawn. Working on paper with a pencil and eraser at this point allows faster adjustments (Photo 1). For instance, you can trace a rose motif as provided in the pattern section of this book directly onto your paper pattern, or you can trace just a portion of the motif if it suits your garment better. Photocopy machines are handy for re-sizing the motifs, if necessary. If you select graphic elements, such as grids, geometric shapes, or other line drawings, you will need to measure, trace, and review placement possibilities as you commit the designs to paper.

4. When you are satisfied with the whole design, permanently record its placement on the paper pattern by using a black, fine-line permanent marker to redraw the lines and shapes or draw around paper templates of the motifs.

5. Cut a square or rectangular piece from your wholecloth fabric, referred to from now on as a fabric section, for each pattern piece. (See Fabric Selection, page 11, to learn about suitable fabrics.) Make the fabric sections large enough to allow about two extra inches for machine stitching or four inches for hand work around the entire pattern. Keep the garment pattern grain line in mind as you work. A square can be used for the whole garment back if there is no seam, while patterns with a front opening fit best on separate rectangles of fabric.

6. Using a light box or window, retrace each of the completed designs onto the right side of the appropriate fabric section with your favorite wash-out marking tool. Remember to trace the outline of the garment shape, too.

7. Continue by following the specific instructions for the project you have selected.

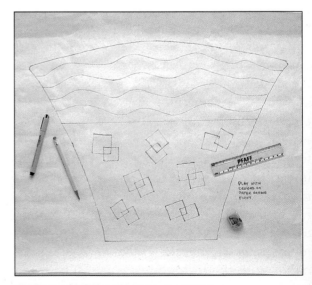

Photo 1: Audition designs on paper.

Advantages of Fabric Sections

Working with fabric sections has definite benefits. They create a built-in margin to allow for take-up caused by the stitching, which is especially important in stipple-quilted garments. The outer edges of the fabric provide ample room for testing stitches before using them in the garment. Frayed seam edges can be avoided by working with marked, uncut fabric pieces. Distortion of bias edges, such as those at the neck and arm holes, can also be prevented. The excess fabric can be used as a "handle" to help you maneuver the piece through the sewing machine or secure it in a hoop for hand quilting, beading or embroidery. Every bit of designing and embellishing can be done on the fabric section before the garment is cut out. Remarking each fabric section with your correct-size, see-through pattern ensures proper placement of the design and reference points for garment assembly (Photo 2).

Advantages of Designing on Paper

Design adjustments can be made on the paper pattern before they are committed to fabric. For instance, stitchers who are fortunate enough to have bountiful chests (or unfortunate depending on your view) may not want a large trapunto rose placed smack in the middle of the breast. For another example, you might need to change the size of the motif. You will notice that in Always Wavering, page 60, there are seven horizontal and seven vertical divisions on a size-10 jumper bodice. If you wear a larger size, you may want to increase the number of divisions or enlarge the design elements in those spaces. It's like working a jigsaw puzzle. You need to add, subtract, and audition various pieces

until everything fits. Just remember to follow the directions and try to think things through. After all the designs have been sewn, place the correct-size, see-through pattern over the stitched fabric (Photo 2). You may need to adjust the pattern placement to accommodate any changes in the position of the design. Use the correct-size pattern as your guide for cutting out the garment piece to guarantee accurate design position and correct garment sizing.

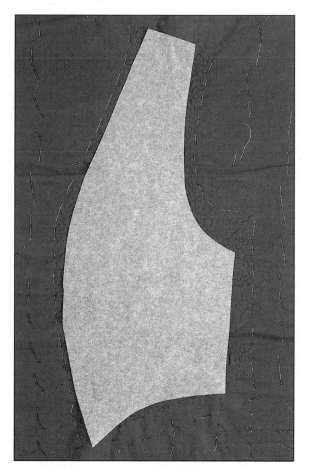

Photo 2: The correct-size pattern is placed on a completed fabric section and used as a cutting guide.

Designing on Fabric

1. Cut a fabric section from your wholecloth fabric for each major garment pattern piece. Cut the fabric section large enough to allow about two inches all around the pattern for machine-stitched designs or four inches for hand work. Be sure to keep the garment pattern's grain line in mind. Any garment pattern pieces, such as collars and facings, that will not be treated with decorative stitching should be cut to the correct size and sewn as usual, following the pattern manufacturer's instructions.

2. Use your favorite wash-out marking tool to trace the outline of all major garment pattern pieces (one-size larger than you normally wear, unless otherwise noted in the pattern) onto the fabric sections. If you are using minimal stitching or a very generous pattern, you may be able to use your correct size.

3. Trace all major pattern pieces in your correct size onto any brand of see-through pattern-tracing material. Cut out the correct-size pattern and retain it to use as a guide when cutting out the garment.

4. Select the desired motifs for the garment and audition their positions on the fabric section. When working with specific shapes, such as stars or lightning bolts, transfer the designs onto freezer paper, cut them out, and play with them within the marked garment boundaries. Photocopy machines are handy for re-sizing motifs. Temporary grid lines or geometric lines can be created by using string or narrow masking tape to check the best placement possibilities (Photo 3).

5. When you are pleased with the arrangement, use your favorite wash-out marking tool to draw the entire design onto the right side of the fabric. Freezer-paper shapes (shiny side down) are easier to draw around if they have been secured to the fabric with the tip of a warm iron. When marking jacket or vest fronts that have mirror images, use a heavy chalk line to mark one side of the garment, including the outline. Place this marked fabric section face up on a firm surface and cover it with the unmarked rectangle for the opposite side, right sides together. Use a brayer or a rolling pin to apply pressure to the fabric sandwich to transfer the chalk onto the companion piece. The markings on each piece may be faint, so you may want to redraw them for better visibility.

6. Continue by following the specific instructions for the project you have selected.

Photo 3: Temporary design lines can be created with masking tape.

Advantages of Designing on Fabric

Working directly on fabric is a real time saver best used for simple designs, such as Tic-Tac Copper Thread, page 44, or paper templates, such as Heat Lightning, page 70. Freezer-paper templates can be pressed onto the fabric, and the fabric section can be held against your body to confirm the positions of the motifs. Grids, and geometric and abstract shapes, can easily be planned and checked before they are permanently sewn. Granted, this method is not precise because you will not be working with fabric cut to size, but it is adequate to give a good impression of the end result. Once all the stitching has been completed, arrange the correct-size, see-through pattern on the fabric section and adjust it to accommodate any changes in the design's location. Use the pattern as a guide to cut out the garment piece. This method will guarantee accurate design positioning and correct garment sizing.

Fabric Selection

In general, solid-color fabrics or those that appear solid will showcase your work the best. The sewing technique you select will impact the fabric choice as well. For example, when you are hand quilting a design from Chapter 1, a quality 100-percent cotton fabric is recommended. On the other hand, the designs in Chapter 3 are best created by using a stabilizing technique, which provides more fabric options. The bodice of Heat Lightning, page 72, was created with silk noil, yet the vest Twice As Nice, page 82, is 100-percent cotton sheeting (Photo 4). Muslin is required for many of the projects. Use a quality 100-percent cotton muslin, prewashed and pressed. Even a steamroller might not be able to get the wrinkles out of inferior muslin. Please read the introductory information in each chapter as a further guide to selecting the appropriate fabric for your wholecloth project.

Photo 4: "Plaid" stitched design is prominent on this solid-color, 100-percent cotton sheeting fabric.

Working on fabric sections often requires slightly more fabric than called for in the garment pattern. A good rule of thumb is to allow an additional one-fourth to one-half yard. To avoid purchasing more fabric than you need, measure how the pattern pieces might fit on the stated yardage, including the two inches for machine stitching or four inches for hand work around the outside of each major piece. Garments with many pattern pieces will often need extra fabric. Those with only two pieces, such as jumper bodices, may not. When figuring your fabric requirements, do not forget to consider the amount you may need for binding, piping or lining. It's a good idea to line your garments with a silky fabric, such as rayon, polyester or silk. Even if it is just in the sleeves, a lining helps you slip the garment on and off more easily.

Batting

Some of the projects in this book were lay-ered with Hobbs Thermore®, a thin polyester batting, which offers several advantages. It is stable, does not require prewashing, will not shrink with laundering, is easy to hand quilt, drapes well, does not add bulk, will not beard, and is readily available. Another ad-vantage is the slightly sticky nature of the batting, which acts almost as a magnet with the fabric. However, there is a drawback to this stickiness when sewing with the batting against the machine bed, because the batting may not feed as smoothly as desired. Many machines can compensate nicely if you use an even-feed foot. You could also try placing paper, even inexpensive notebook paper, or a tear-away stabilizer between the batting and the feed dogs. You could also consider adding a muslin layer to your fabric section.

Equipment Needed

Sewing Machine

In an effort to help you avoid too much trial and error, the project directions are as com-plete as possible. When appropriate, machine settings are provided in generic terms. You will need to experiment to confirm the exact settings for your machine. A fancy computer-ized machine is not a necessity. As long as your machine is capable of sewing a zigzag stitch, you will be able to re-create all but one of the machine-stitched designs. Using a walking or even-feed foot helps to avoid distorted or puckered fabric. If your machine is not equipped with a walking foot, check your local sewing center for a generic attachment, which is usually available at a nominal cost. Before committing to your project, always test stitch-es in the margin of your fabric to confirm

thread color, thread performance, needle size, tension settings, and visual impact.

Light Box

Many of the designs provided require trac-ing, either onto a paper pattern or the fabric itself. Quilters are often faced with tracing tasks, and most people are familiar with the procedure of taping motifs to a window to make their tracings. Obstacles arise with detailed or large drawings or with dark, thick or dense material. To solve these problems, you may want to purchase a light box. They are available through a number of mail-order sewing catalogs, and art, photography or graphic-design supply stores. Purchase one with the largest surface you can afford to avoid repeated repositioning of the designs. You can also use a light box that was origi-nally intended for viewing slides. The bulb does not get hot, and the light penetrates so well that you can see through fabrics that have been layered with batting. Although this equipment is not mandatory, if you become intrigued with these methods, you might con-sider owning one.

Marking Tools

Always use a marking pen or pencil that is removable yet has high visibility. Be sure to test the product before marking on your pro-ject. There are many variables affecting the satisfactory use of marking tools. The stabi-lizing methods vary and so does the amount of handling the fabric receives. Fabrics might need to be subjected to high heat, steam, and even laundering to remove the stabilizer. These processes can potentially cause the markings to fade with time or rub off, and some markers can even stain permanently.

If the water supply for your home is a private well, you might not be able to remove some of the washable chalk or pencil marks because of a chemical reaction with the water. Marking with slivers of ordinary bar soap can be effective in this situation. Most any brand will do; however, some of the moisturizing ones tend to crumble. Using deodorant soaps has not caused problems in staining or washing out, but again, you need to test all marking tools on all your fabrics before using them. Admittedly, a soap sliver is not as precise as a sharp pencil, but it is effective for all but the most intricate designs. Many designs do not require extreme accuracy. If the shape of a traced fern is a little off, does it really matter? Nature is not perfect either. You will be amazed at how well soap shows up on fabric, even on very light-colored material. When a complex thin line is needed, you can switch to a mechanical soapstone pencil. Unfortunately, maintaining a nice pointed tip on soapstone is not easy, and you need firm pressure to make the line visible.

Embellishments

Embellishments can play an important role in your garment. With the exception of some simple embroidery, beading is the only type of embellishment used for the projects in this book (see Elementary Beading on page 14). Naturally, charms, trinkets, buttons, ribbons or whatever items your creativity conjures up would be welcome additions. Be sure to use quality materials and sew them on, rather than glue them (Photo 5).

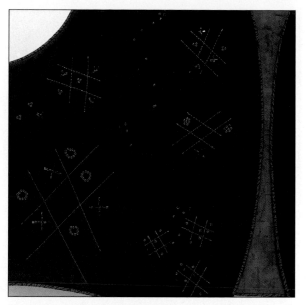

Photo 5: Tic-Tac Copper Thread Vest (detail). Beading was used to enhance the stitching pattern. (Project begins on page 44.)

As you have probably gathered, there is a lot of "wiggle room" in the way I go about creating my garments. Often, more time can be spent getting ready to sew than in actually sewing the garment, and I've learned that proper planning and preparation can help avoid disappointments. "Mistakes" are inevitable, but I prefer to think of them as design opportunities!

Elementary Beading

Here are a few suggestions to get you acquainted with some elementary beading techniques. This is just an introduction, so if you are new to beading, do not hesitate to seek out the myriad of books, magazines, and workshops available for further information.

• Stitch beads onto the fabric section after the design has been sewn but before the garment is cut out. Beading can draw up the fabric in a manner similar to quilting.

• Secure fabric in a hoop to maintain proper tension and avoid puckering.

• Use either white, black or gray beading thread. Select the color that best blends with the bead.

• Work with lengths of thread no more than about 15 inches long to prevent the thread from wearing and fraying.

• Use a #10 or #12 quilting needle.

• Good quality beads are a must. Ragged edges on bugle beads, for instance, can cut the thread.

• Always test the colorfastness of your beads by soaking them in hot water and detergent. Be aware that chemicals used for dry cleaning can affect the color and general appearance of some types of beads.

• Use the illustrations, Steps 1-5, as a guide for adding beads to your garments.

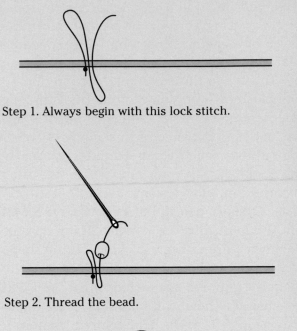

Step 1. Always begin with this lock stitch.

Step 2. Thread the bead.

Step 3. To stitch the bead, place the needle into the fabric on the opposite side of the bead, covering up the lock stitch.

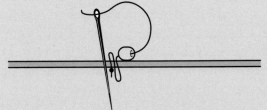

Step 4. To stitch lines of beads, bring the needle up one bead length away from the first bead, string the next bead, and put the needle down through the fabric beside the first bead. This perle stitch is similar to a backstitch.

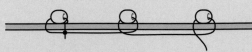

Step 5. You can use the perle stitch for a scattered effect by traveling under the fabric for 1" to 1½" between beads. It's best not to travel more than this distance between beads.

Stipple Quilting and Trapunto

Since early colonial days, wholecloth, solid-color quilts displaying intricate and finely stitched patterns have been highly prized. Quilts created with white cotton fabric and thread became known as "white-work quilts" or "white on white." These elegant quilts featured elaborate quilting motifs, abundant with feathers, leaves, baskets, and flowers. They often displayed stuffed areas, called trapunto, that were further emphasized by their closely stipple-quilted backgrounds. Such quilts often took years to complete and were generally attempted by only the most experienced stitchers.

The projects in this chapter feature motifs specifically designed to produce raised surface textures created by cording or stuffing the stitched designs. The motifs were sized to be compatible with a variety of garment styles. All but the first project include a stipple-quilted background. Most of the methods offered are applicable to either hand or machine quilting.

Acquaint yourself with the following general instructions and refer to them as necessary during the construction of your wholecloth garment. Because the designs vary, recommendations covering the process of adapting them to your individual garment can be found in the text for each project.

Fabric Suggestions

Select a solid-color fabric to best showcase the designs (Photo 6). As you can see in Photo 7,

an attempt to use a beautiful hand-dyed cotton was unsuccessful. Fabric selection can also be influenced by how easy the material is to hand quilt. Look for medium-weight, 100-percent cotton fabric. Avoid thin and loosely woven material because it will not support the rigors of stuffing or stipple quilting, and small hand-quilting stitches have a tendency to get lost between the fibers. Pass up heavy, dense fabrics, such as cotton sheeting, canvas, and denim. They are difficult to needle and too stiff to drape nicely when stipple quilted. Natural fibers, such as light-weight wools, linen, and even some medium-weight blends can be considered, but be sure to do some test stitching before committing to an entire

Photo 6: Solid-color fabric will provide the best visual impact for trapunto and stipple-quilted projects.

garment. You can use 100-percent cotton muslin for the backing, which will be hidden by the lining in the finished garment. A similar quality, woven cotton fabric from your stash that's no longer appealing is a suitable alternative to muslin. Prewash all washable fabrics and press them before beginning.

Photo 7: Both the texture and the design are almost completely lost on mottled fabric.

Preparing for Stitching

Transfer your chosen trapunto design to the right side of the appropriate fabric section. Cut a piece of a high quality, prewashed and pressed 100-percent cotton muslin and a piece of batting, both identical in size to the fabric section. At the corners and in the middle of each side, tape the muslin piece to a firm surface. Cover the muslin with the piece of batting, followed by the fabric section with the marked side facing up. Thread baste the layers together vertically and horizontally every two or three inches. Closely baste the outline of the garment shape so it is distinguishable in case the marking lines are rubbed off.

After removing the tape from the muslin, the layered section is ready for stitching. Repeat for each pattern piece. The batting has a dual role in trapunto. It acts as a stabilizer and gives depth to the stitches. The muslin is used as an underlining to provide a foundation for the stuffing.

Thread Choices

Hand basting with an economical white basting thread eliminates any possibility of the thread's dye transferring to the fabric. Dye transfer can be caused by humidity in the air, perspiration from one's hands, and just the passing of time.

Naturally, when you are hand quilting, a strong thread made specifically for that purpose is always a good choice. Whenever possible, match the thread color to the fabric to ensure that the impact of the design will not be overpowered by the thread. To camouflage the size of your quilting stitches, you can use a finer thread.

Solid-color specialty threads can also be attractive. Use 40-weight rayon and metallic threads for hand quilting and 30-weight for machine stitching. Be aware that these threads are more fragile and prone to fraying and breaking. Hand stitching with shorter lengths, about 15 inches long, can help to avoid some of these problems.

Notice in Photo 8 how the small quilting stitches sewn with metallic thread provide tiny sparks of light without detracting from the design. However, the outcome would not have been as positive with large quilting stitches. Always test your thread selection before beginning your project to be sure the results are effective. The size of your quilting stitches, the garment style, and the desired motifs will influence the overall appearance of the finished piece.

Photo 8: Small quilting stitches of copper metallic thread add sparkle to the design.

Stipple Quilting

On hearing the word "stipple," one automatically thinks of zillions of stitches. Stipple quilting requires a lot of stitching, but it's not just the stitches that create the look we love. It's the wrinkles and creases that are formed in the small areas between the stitches that provide texture, and texture is what stippling is really about. Stipple quilting also flattens the fabric around corded and stuffed areas, accentuating the raised design. The stitching is most effective when a solid fabric and matching thread are used, because the pattern in a print fabric would camouflage the stitches, and a highly contrasting thread would overpower the subtle designs. In other words, the texture you desire would not be as evident.

Hand Stippling

Using a hoop or frame for hand quilting is recommended because they help to reduce distortion and ensure a pucker-free garment. Begin by quilting the outlines of the designs while the traced lines are distinct. You can then stipple quilt all open areas except the seam allowances.

Some of the well-known patterns used for hand stipple quilting, such as checkerboard, diamond, and herringbone, don't translate well to clothing because of the interruption of seam lines, collars, front openings, and sleeves. Echo stipple quilting is similar to echo quilting; that is, the stitches are worked around a motif in concentric lines, but they are spaced much closer together, about one-eighth inch apart. This stipple pattern tends to distort smaller garment pieces, especially if you have a tight quilting stitch.

My favorite stipple quilting pattern (non-pattern really) is a meandering line, because it doesn't require matching pattern lines at the seams. To be authentic, it should be a continuous line. Mine aren't all the time, but who'd ever know?

Once the garment is assembled, the stipple-quilted areas will flow together beautifully, allowing the featured motifs to play their starring role. The meandering pattern is more forgiving for filling in the background areas of small or intricate motifs with denser stitching (Photo 9, page 18).

Stippling is done free-hand, without marking the pattern onto the fabric. You'll undoubtedly feel very indecisive about which direction to go at first, but that will be overcome with time and practice. In Fig. 1, notice how the squiggly pattern resembles a jigsaw puzzle. If it makes you more comfortable, go ahead and mark some lines to follow at first. Keep those puzzle shapes in your mind as you stitch, sewing them about a scant one-fourth inch apart. A mistake most novices make with clothing is to pack the quilting lines too close together, which flattens and stiffens the garment and reduces its drape.

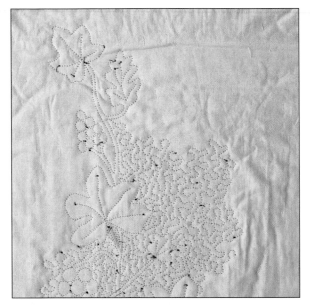

Photo 9: Meander stipple quilting is shown in progress, as seen from the muslin (back) side.

Beginning and ending knots can be made on the muslin side, which will be covered by the lining. It's easiest to begin stitching in a corner or a tight area and work toward the open areas (Fig. 2). You may find that the meandering lines need to be stitched closer together in some areas to help distinguish them from the motif. Work the pattern around itself rather than stitching perpendicular to a design or working in rows (Fig. 3 a-c). Another key to successful stippling is changing directions often.

Quilting oneself into a corner is frequently unavoidable. Hand quilters normally let the

needle travel through the batting to a new location, but be careful not to travel through areas that will have trapunto (Fig. 4).

Meandering quilting doesn't permit the gathering of several stitches on your needle at a

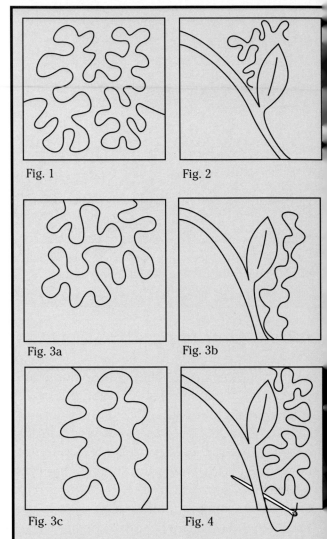

Fig. 1   Fig. 2

Fig. 3a   Fig. 3b

Fig. 3c   Fig. 4

Fig. 1: Stipple quilting produces a jigsaw puzzle effect.

Fig. 2: Begin stipple quilting in a tight area and work toward open spaces.

Fig. 3: Work the pattern around itself (a), rather than stitching perpendicular to the design (b) or working in rows (c).

Fig. 4: Do not travel across areas to be stuffed.

time. To achieve gentle curves, you will need to take only two stitches at a time and pull them through. Sometimes, even one stitch at a time is required.

Machine Stippling

For machine quilting, fabric sandwiches can be basted with small safety pins, or you may want to use a no-baste machine quilting frame (see Products and Sources, page 102).

Machine quilting has a tendency to produce fabric with less drape. Therefore, fabrics heavier than medium-weight cotton are not recommended. Because machine stippling creates more stiffness in the fabric than hand quilting, try to sew the stipple lines at least one-fourth inch apart. Narrow areas won't permit this tactic but attempt it wherever possible.

The quilting design will be more apparent if the needle is threaded with a color that matches the garment or with invisible nylon thread. You can use lightweight cotton thread in the bobbin.

Before you begin sewing, carefully examine the stitching order to avoid unnecessary starts and stops. Test your stitching on the outside edges of the fabric section before beginning to quilt on the garment. Secure thread ends at the beginning and end of each line by sewing six or eight stitches with the stitch length set near but not on zero. You can use an automatic tie-off function if the needle moves forward and back rather than stitching in place, or you can pull the threads through to the back and tie them.

Basic Trapunto

The terms trapunto, Italian trapunto and padded appliqué, along with such descriptions as corded, stuffed, and padded, are commonly used interchangeably, although they encompass several different techniques. Two methods, trapunto and corded trapunto, will be described for use with the projects in this book.

The basic trapunto process involves stitching the outline of a motif, such as a flower or leaf, and stuffing it for a padded, sculptural effect (Photos 10 & 11). For quiltmaking, this method was traditionally accomplished by gently spreading apart the threads of a coarsely woven backing and inserting bits of batting into the design until the area was sufficiently raised. A stiletto was often used for this task to help work the holes closed after each area was filled. The process is much easier for garment making because the holes in the muslin layer, which will be hidden by a lining, can be cut with embroidery scissors.

Photo 10: The design has less impact before stipple quilting and trapunto have been completed.

Stipple Quilting and Trapunto

Begin working on the trapunto after all outline and stipple quilting have been completed. The stipple-quilted background provides stability around the areas to be stuffed and helps prevent the tendency to overfill the motifs.

Remove the garment section from your hoop or frame before beginning trapunto. Working from the back, use a small, sharp embroidery scissors to cut a small slit in the muslin behind the motif. The fabric will fray less and offer less resistance during filling if it is cut on the bias (Fig. 5). Do not cut into the batting or wholecloth fabric. Complicated motifs may require slits in each section of the design to make stuffing easier.

Insert a small amount of stuffing material, such as a polyester filling (not quilt batting) with a blunt tapestry needle, crochet hook, stiletto, or one of the specialty stuffing tools available. Continue stuffing small bits at a time until the motif is lightly but evenly filled (Fig. 6). Do not overstuff! Overfilling causes the background around the design to distort and pucker. This problem is more apparent if the background has not been stipple quilted. Whip stitch the opening closed (Fig. 7).

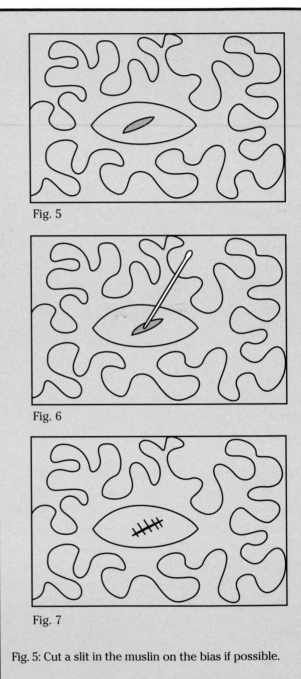

Fig. 5

Fig. 6

Fig. 7

Fig. 5: Cut a slit in the muslin on the bias if possible.

Fig. 6: Use a blunt needle to insert stuffing material.

Fig. 7: Close the opening with whip stitching.

Photo 11: The texture of stipple quilting combined with the stuffed leaves enhances the design.

Corded Trapunto

This method is handy for filling narrow areas such as stems, vines, and cables. Lengths of cotton or synthetic yarn are used for stuffing instead of batting (Photo 12). Because the design scale is often reduced on garments, you will find this technique helpful for stuffing some of the smaller motifs, such as wheat stalks, rosebuds, and fern fronds.

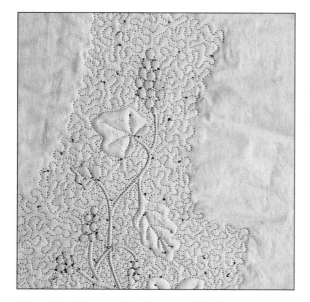

Photo 12: Vines and grapes are filled with yarn, as seen on the back of a completed fabric section.

A blunt tapestry, crewel, or yarn needle can be used for corded trapunto. Look for one with a large eye to make threading the yarn easier. Long trapunto needles are useful for stuffing lengthy straight channels but are too cumbersome to maneuver through curvy designs. A #16 yarn darner, which has a slightly pointed tip, makes it easier to pierce the muslin.

Take the time to experiment to find the appropriate yarn size to achieve well-executed cording for your specific project. If the yarn is too narrow, the overall impact of the design will be reduced, yet cording with yarn that is too thick will cause distortion of the background fabric. Try a variety of yarns, everything from acrylic baby yarn to heavier rug yarns, depending on the design to be filled. The yarn strand can be doubled for wider channels.

Even though the yarn is under the batting, attempt to match the yarn color to the fabric to prevent any possibility of shadowing. To avoid making the fabric too stiff, refrain from using heavy cording material.

Begin corded trapunto after all outline and stipple quilting have been completed. Remove the garment section from your hoop or frame. Working from the back side, insert a needle, threaded with yarn, through the muslin layer and run it through the channel created by the stitches. Leave at least a two-inch tail at the beginning to ensure that no gap will be created if you tug too hard and pull more yarn through than you intended.

Manipulate the needle through the design by gathering as much of the channel onto the needle as possible as you go. Bring the needle out where the design turns or where it becomes difficult to proceed (Fig. 8, page 22). Pull the yarn through the motif, leaving it slightly slack to ensure pucker-free lines. Continue cording by reinserting the needle into the same hole. Adjust the slack in the strand of yarn as you go. When the motif has been completely filled, trim the yarn ends close to the fabric.

Finishing and Assembly

Press each fabric section from the wrong side with a pressing cloth and enough steam and pressure to remove any wrinkles, which may be most apparent on the outside edges of your marked pattern. Do your best not to flatten the trapunto.

With the pressed fabric section right side up, place the correct-size pattern on top. The see-through pattern will allow better visibility so you can correctly position the pattern shape over the stitched design. Feel free to move the pattern up, down or sideways if you feel the design placement needs to be adjusted. Notice that the fabric section marked with the larger pattern has shrunk and is nearer to your correct size. When satisfied with the placement, re-mark the outline of the garment on the fabric.

Check to see if any quilting stitches extend beyond the newly marked cutting line. If so, secure them by machine stay-stitching in the seam allowance. Any areas adjacent to seams that require more quilting can be stitched after the garment has been sewn together but before the facings and lining are added.

Cut out the garment pieces and assemble them according to the pattern manufacturer's instructions. To reduce bulk in the seams, trim the muslin and batting seam allowances wherever possible and press them open.

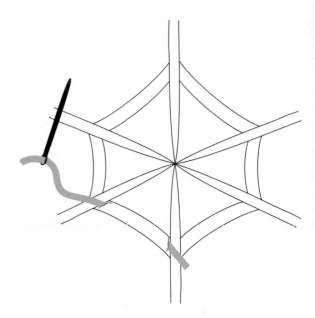

Fig. 8. Bring the needle out where the design changes direction.

Caught in the Web

The vest shown on page 24 was made with 100-percent cotton fabric. It features spider-web motifs, which have been hand quilted with cotton-covered polyester quilting thread and corded to emphasize the design. Spider-web designs were often embroidered on Victorian crazy quilts as a symbol of good luck. The vest is fairly quick to make because the background is not quilted, so it's a good choice to begin exploring the methods offered in this chapter. Naturally, to achieve more design definition, the background area could be stipple quilted, if desired.

Designing and Sewing

1. Select your vest pattern.

2. Follow the instructions for designing on paper, page 8, and the Stori Lines for the Caught in the Web pattern, page 26.

3. Create a fabric sandwich for each garment section by thread basting as described in the introduction to this chapter.

4. Outline quilt spider-web designs through all three layers. Take special care to avoid pulling the quilting thread too tight or the unquilted areas may become distorted.

5. Use the corded trapunto technique described on page 21 to stuff the webs.

6. If desired, use a simple outline embroidery stitch to add a few spiders while the fabric can still be secured in a hoop (Photo 13).

7. If necessary, block the fabric sections by lightly pressing them with steam.

8. Keeping the design elements and seam allowances in mind, position your correct-size,

continued on page 26

Photo 13: Caught in the Web vest and detail. The spider was hand embroidered with an outline stitch.

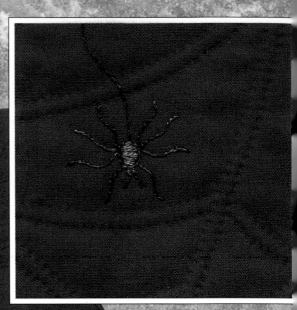

The Wholecloth Garment Stori

Stori Line Creations
Caught in the Web

Here are some examples of how the web patterns can be used to fit various garments. (Please note that, in these drawings, the designs may have been altered, reversed, or combined.) The letters refer to full-size, ready-to-trace patterns on the large lift-out sheets accompanying this book.

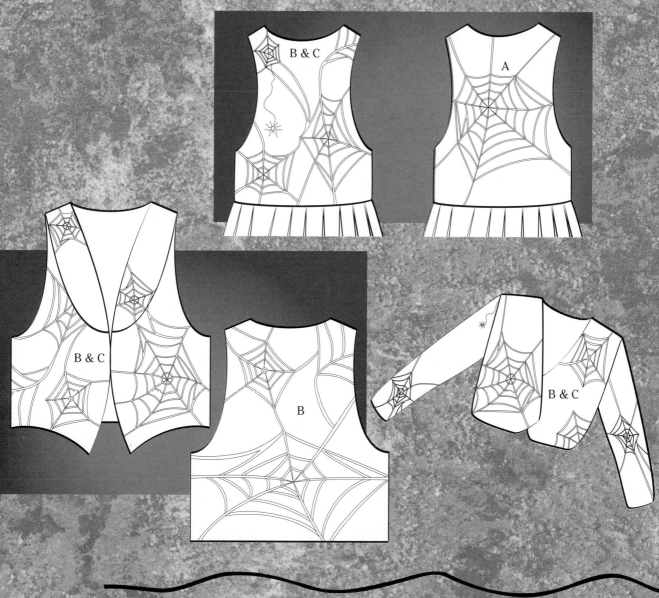

see-through patterns on the quilted and cord-ed fabric sections. Re-mark the garment cut-ting lines.

9. Machine stay-stitch just outside the seam line, around each garment shape, to secure the batting and any hand-quilting stitches in the seam allowances.

10. Cut out all the garment pieces. Sew them together, following the pattern manufacturer's directions. Don't forget to grade the allow-ances and press them open to reduce bulk.

11. Check to be sure that all the connecting lines that run into the seam allowances have been completely quilted and stuffed. Additional quilting may be required if the pattern shape was repositioned when it was re-marked.

12. Complete the vest with a lining.

Photo 14: Caught in the Web vest (back view).

Caught in the Web Stori Lines

Unless your garment is very fitted, the paper pattern can be drawn using your correct size for this design. However, if you are unsure of the fit, use the one size larger pattern.

Study the garment layout for the vest, top of page 25, and compare it to your garment pattern. Determine which designs might best fit your garment pieces. Reposition and play with the design as needed. Don't be impatient. This part will take more than half an hour.

If the designs don't fit as provided, consider either adding more lines to the outside of a web to enlarge it or eliminating some to reduce the size.

Connector lines between the motifs help the designs work together. If the ones shown won't translate to your garment shape, draw new ones. Remember, you aren't creating a Mariner's Compass block. When was the last time you saw a perfect spider web?

Draw connector lines at least an inch or two away from each other at the seam so it doesn't appear as if you attempted to have them match and didn't quite make it.

It isn't necessary to place as many webs on your garment as shown in the sample. For a quicker approach, consider stitching one large web on the back and perhaps just one on each front panel.

In your drawing, be sure to extend some of the connector lines to run through any large unquilted areas to hold the batting in place.

Keep the width of any new channel lines you create approximately the same distance apart as the orig-inal designs.

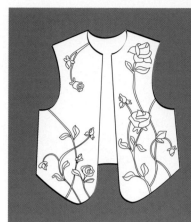

Pretty & Pink

A medium-weight rayon and polyester fabric was chosen for this Pretty & Pink jumper bodice shown on page 28, primarily because the fabric coordinated with the linen skirt better than the 100-percent cotton counterparts. To provide a visual example of the flexibility these designs offer, this garment was machine stipple quilted by Alex Dupré, a fellow wearable-art and quilt instructor. Alex used 30-weight rayon thread in the needle and a lightweight bobbin thread. I added the trapunto and the piping when I assembled the jumper. Hand quilters will want to use a traditional quilting thread that matches their fabric.

Designing and Sewing

1. Select your jumper pattern.

2. Follow the instructions for designing on paper, page 8, and the Stori Lines for the Pretty & Pink pattern, page 30.

3. Create a fabric sandwich for each garment section. Hand quilters may want to thread baste. Machine quilters can pin baste.

4. Outline quilt the designs through all three layers. Where one motif overlaps another, stitch the outline of the top motif first. For the bottom motif, stop quilting when you reach the outline of the top one and lock stitch or tie off the threads. Resume quilting on the other side of the top motif. For channels that will have cording, take care that there is enough space between the stitched lines for the yarn to pass through. Sometimes these lines get closer together then originally drawn because of the thickness of the marking tool.

5. Stipple quilt all open areas, up to the seam allowances.

6. Use polyester filling and cording to fill the

continued on page 30

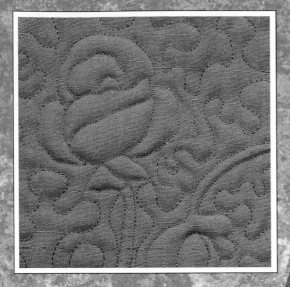

Photo 15: Pretty & Pink jumper (and detail), designed and constructed by the author, and machine quilted by Alex Dupré.

Stori Line Creations
Pretty & Pink

Here are some examples of how the Pretty & Pink patterns can be used to fit various garments. (Please note that, in these drawings, the designs may have been altered, reversed, or combined.) The letters refer to full-size, ready-to-trace patterns on the large lift-out sheets accompanying this book.

Photo 16: Pretty & Pink jumper (detail), trapunto by the author. Alex Dupré machine stipple quilted this design with 30-weight rayon thread.

motifs, following the trapunto instructions on page 19.

7. Block the fabric sections by steam pressing them carefully.

8. Position your correct-size, see-through patterns on the quilted and stuffed fabric sections, keeping the design elements and seam allowances in mind. When satisfied with the placement, re-mark the pattern cutting lines.

9. Machine stay-stitch just outside the seam line, around each garment shape, to secure the batting and any hand-quilting stitches in the seam allowances.

10. Cut out all the garment pieces. Assemble them following your pattern manufacturer's directions. Don't forget to grade the allowances and press them open to reduce bulk.

11. If the pattern shape was repositioned when marked, additional stipple quilting may be required near the seams.

12. Complete the garment with a lining and enjoy this very wearable jumper!

Pretty & Pink Stori Lines

Trace major pattern pieces one size larger for this project.

Keep important design elements, such as the rosebud, about an inch away from the seam allowances to avoid lopping off part of the flower when the garment is cut to size.

If the designs don't fit as provided, consider either adding to or subtracting from any of the motifs, or placing the compositions on the pattern at a slight angle.

Amber Waves of Grain

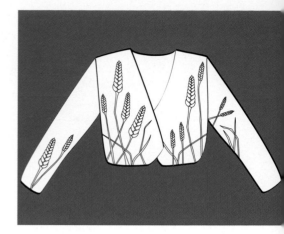

Since drawing is not a skill I possess, finding appropriate wheat stalk motifs that would translate to garments turned out to be a challenge. My long search finally paid off when I located some possibilities in a cookbook. After a little enlarging on my photocopy machine and time spent simplifying some of the lines, the designing went smoothly.

A commercially dyed medium-weight, 100-percent brushed cotton fabric was selected for the vest on page 32. The slightly mottled color gives the appearance of soft leather, yet it is not distracting because the color still reads as a solid. It was quilted with a cotton-covered, polyester hand-quilting thread in a matching color. The partial shawl collar (each end is stitched into the shoulder seam) has its own facing, allowing the trapunto to be accomplished invisibly. A collarless vest pattern would be perfectly adaptable for this project.

Designing and Sewing

1. Select your vest pattern.

2. Follow the instructions for designing on paper, page 8, and the Stori Lines for the Amber Waves of Grain pattern, page 35.

3. Outline quilt the designs through all three layers. Noting that some motifs overlap others will help you to avoid accidentally sewing across the top motif. The stems require that you stitch channels to create areas for the cording. Sometimes these lines get closer together then originally drawn because of the thickness of the marking tool, so take care that there is enough space between them to allow the yarn to pass through.

4. The main vest pattern pieces are stipple quilted through all three layers before they are filled. Do not stipple quilt in the seam allowances.

5. Fill the motifs by following the trapunto instructions on page 19.

6. Block the fabric sections by carefully steam pressing them.

continued on page 34

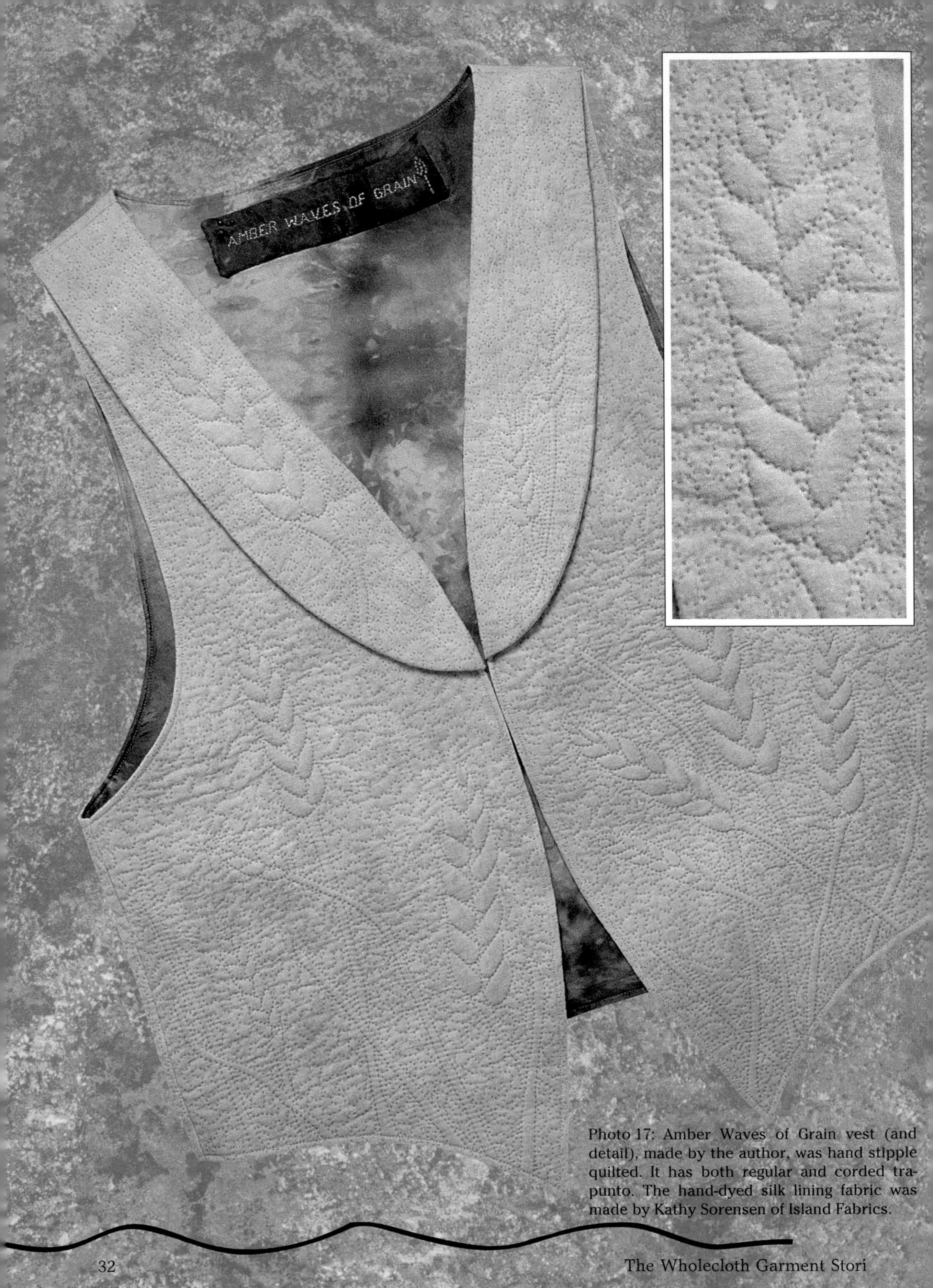

Photo 17: Amber Waves of Grain vest (and detail), made by the author, was hand stipple quilted. It has both regular and corded trapunto. The hand-dyed silk lining fabric was made by Kathy Sorensen of Island Fabrics.

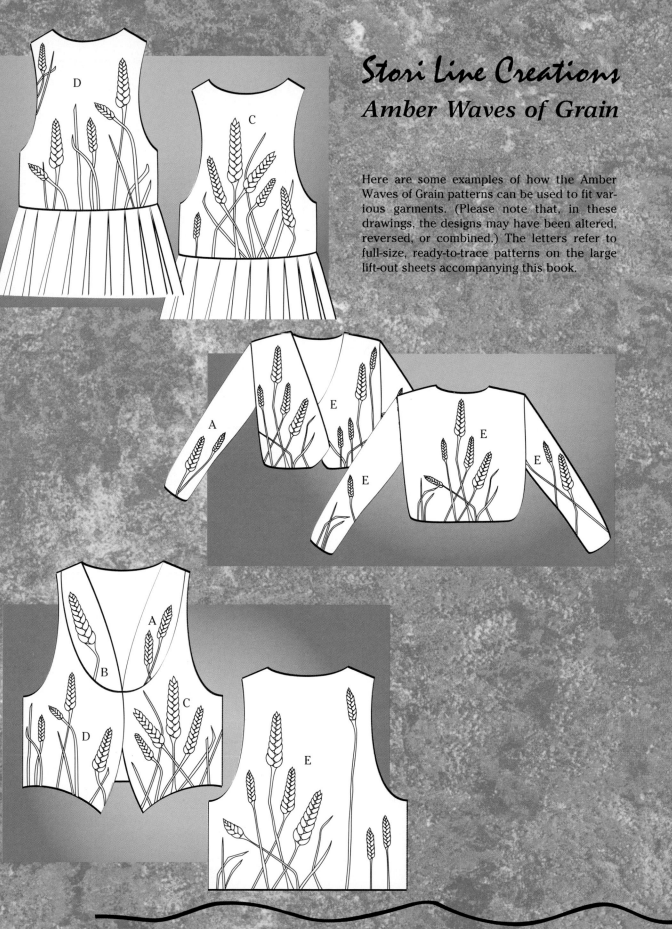

Stori Line Creations
Amber Waves of Grain

Here are some examples of how the Amber Waves of Grain patterns can be used to fit various garments. (Please note that, in these drawings, the designs may have been altered, reversed, or combined.) The letters refer to full-size, ready-to-trace patterns on the large lift-out sheets accompanying this book.

7. Keep the design elements and seam allowances in mind as you position the correct-size, see-through garment patterns on all the quilted and stuffed fabric sections. When satisfied with the placement, re-mark the pattern cutting lines on the fabric.

8. Machine stay-stitch just outside the seam line, around each garment shape, to secure the batting and any hand-quilting stitches in the seam allowances.

9. Cut out all the garment pieces. Sew them together, following the pattern manufacturer's directions. Don't forget to grade the allowances and press them open to reduce bulk.

10. If the pattern shape was repositioned when marked, additional stipple quilting may be required near the seams.

11. Complete the vest with a lining.

Collars with Separate Facings

Use the following method for collars that are constructed with their own separate facing, not for patterns that have a combination collar and vest facing pattern piece:

Outline quilt the design through all three layers. Stuff the motifs. Since these are smaller-scale designs, use the cording technique for stuffing, rather than cutting a slit into such small areas and trying to add filling. Notice that stuffing before stippling is a deviation from the normal procedure. Because the background hasn't been stipple quilted yet, you'll need to be very careful not to overfill.

Use a small sharp embroidery scissors to trim away the excess muslin in all areas except those that are filled, leaving about a one-eighth-inch edging of muslin around the outside of all corded motifs. Trimming away the excess muslin reduces bulk, producing more professional-looking results. This method is best used on small pieces for which a minimum of trapunto or cording is required. It is not recommended for large pattern pieces.

Stipple quilt all the open areas in the collar. You will be quilting through only two layers, the top and the batting. When the garment is assembled, the collar facing will finish the back of this piece.

Photo 18: Amber Waves of Grain vest (back view and detail).

Amber Waves of Grain Stori Lines

Trace major pattern pieces one size larger for this project. If your pattern has a partial collar, it's necessary to trace only the collar pattern piece, not the facing.

Keep important design elements, like the wheat grains, about an inch away from the seam allowances to avoid lopping off part of the design when the garment is cut to size.

If the designs don't fit as provided, consider either adding to or subtracting from any of the motifs. For instance, the length of the wheat stalks could be lengthened or shortened to fit the size of your vest. Placing the motifs closer or farther apart or positioning the compositions at a slight angle on the pattern are other methods for making adjustments.

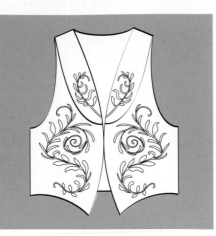

Spring Green

The dressy jacket shown on the facing page and on page 38 provides a lovely way to show off your quilting skills. Though it appears quite elegant, its humble beginning was a solid forest green, 100-percent cotton woven fabric. It was hand quilted with a matching green cotton-covered, polyester hand-quilting thread. The beading wasn't originally planned, but a new stash of iridescent tri-cut beads generated a new direction and quickly elevated this jacket for those more formal occasions. The beads, of course, are not mandatory. Skip them if you prefer a less formal garment.

Designing and Sewing

1. Select your jacket pattern. Look for a collarless jacket that includes facings. Collars and garment edges finished with seam binding may detract from the overall effect of this design.

2. Follow the instructions for designing on paper, page 8, and the Stori Lines for the Spring Green pattern, page 37. Trace major pattern pieces one size larger for this project, excluding facings.

3. Create a fabric sandwich for each garment section by thread basting as described in the introduction to this chapter.

4. Outline quilt the designs through all three layers. The main branches of the ferns require that channels be stitched for cording. Sometimes these lines get closer together than originally drawn because of the thickness of the marking tool, so take care that there is enough space between them to allow yarn to pass through.

5. Stipple quilt all open areas on each pattern piece, up to the seam allowances.

6. Fill the motifs, following the basic trapun-

to and cording instructions on pages 20–21.

7. Block the fabric sections by carefully steam pressing them.

8. If beading is planned, do it while the fabric sections can still be secured in a hoop. Keep beads at least two inches from all seam lines to prevent breakage when the jacket is assembled. Be sure to give the sections a good pressing before beading because it's more difficult to do it once the beads are in place. A light pressing may still be required after the beads are added. Use a terry-cloth towel to protect them.

9. Position your correct-size, see-through garment pattern pieces on the quilted and stuffed fabric sections, keeping the design elements and seam allowances in mind. When satisfied with the placement, re-mark the pattern cutting lines.

10. Machine stay-stitch, just outside the seam line, around each garment shape, to secure the hand-quilting stitches.

11. Cut out all the garment pieces. Assemble them following your pattern manufacturer's directions. Don't forget to grade the allowances and press them open to reduce bulk.

12. If the pattern shape was repositioned when marked, additional stipple quilting may be required near the seams.

13. Add a lining to complete the jacket.

Photo 19: Spring Green jacket (back view).

Spring Green Stori Lines

Notice that the garment pictured on page 38 has an asymmetrical front closure. Some adjustments may be required to adapt the fern designs to fit the front sections of a classic-style jacket.

You will need to plan sleeve motifs for the first time. Just as in other pattern pieces, remember to keep important design elements away from the seam and hem allowances.

If the designs don't fit as provided, consider either adding to or subtracting from any of the motifs. Modify curves if necessary, too. Nature doesn't feature perfectly shaped greenery. Adjustments can also be made by positioning the compositions on the pattern at a slight angle.

Photo 20: Spring Green jacket (detail) was beaded by hand with tri-cut iridescent beads.

Photo 21: Spring Green jacket, made by the author, was hand stipple quilted. It has trapunto and corded trapunto. For the satin lining, the author used textile paint, and live ferns as stencils.

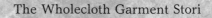

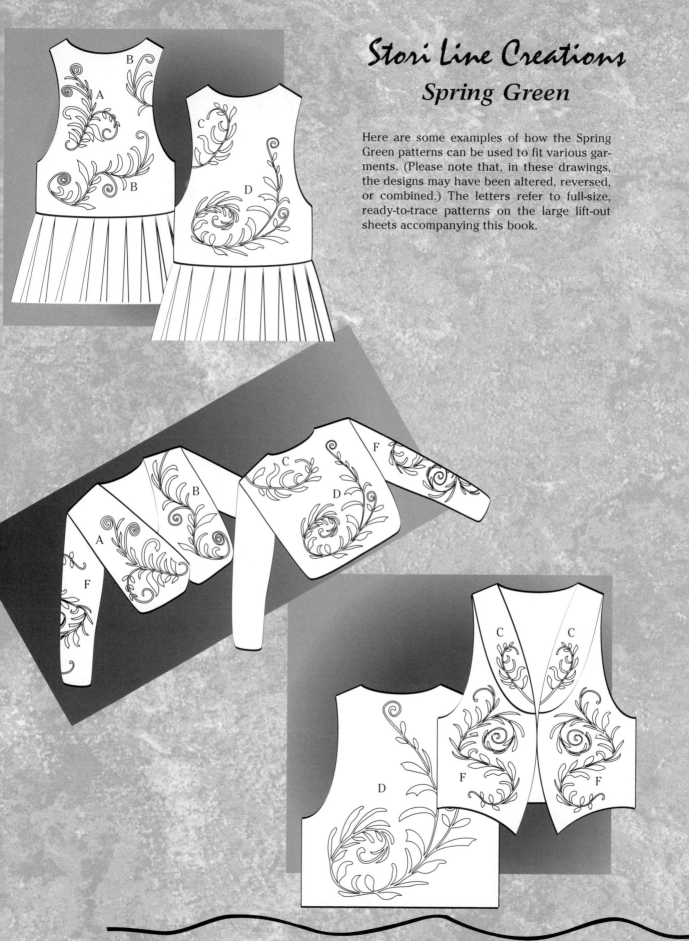

Stori Line Creations
Spring Green

Here are some examples of how the Spring Green patterns can be used to fit various garments. (Please note that, in these drawings, the designs may have been altered, reversed, or combined.) The letters refer to full-size, ready-to-trace patterns on the large lift-out sheets accompanying this book.

Chapter 2

Machine Quilting

The machine quilting method used for the designs in this chapter is not free-motion, and you will not need to use a machine-quilting hoop. The technique requires only a straight or zigzag stitch, which anyone with a machine that zigzags can sew. This unconventional method yields innovative results not normally associated with machine quilting. Yet, the process technically is quilting because the stitched layers include batting, which adds stability, warmth, texture, and definition to the piece. The projects incorporate a variety of fabrics, designs, and thread choices to expose you to different approaches. Before beginning, thoroughly read the instructions for the project you have selected. It will not be long before you are quickly and easily creating unique, wearable garments by varying the fabric, stitch length and width, and type of thread.

Photo 22: Running Parallel jacket, made by the author and modeled by Whitney Schroeder. The cotton chambray was stabilized to eliminate the need to work in a hoop for machine quilting.

Fabric and Stabilizing Suggestions

It is important to prewash and press yardage before starting your project. After washing, which removes the commercially applied sizing, the fabric may need to be stabilized for machine quilting. Stabilizing may be as simple as adding batting because fabrics have a tendency to cling to some types of batting. You may want to test this method before taking what might be unnecessary further steps.

Basting with thread or small safety pins is still necessary, but you will be able to eliminate the need to work in a hoop, which some people find extremely frustrating. Stiffening fabrics with starch first will expand the variety of fabrics that can be quilted by machine, including silk noil, rayon and silk blends, linen and cotton blends, traditional quilters' cottons, lightweight cotton sheeting, and chambray, to name a few. Always test a small fabric sample to check for color changes and spotting before starching large sections.

Obviously, the weight and the fiber content will be factors in how the fabric behaves during the machine-quilting process. Medium-weight, closely woven fabrics, or those stiffened by paints or dyes, can usually be stabilized adequately with batting alone. The only way to know for sure is to test before you begin.

Heavy fabrics, such as dense, stiff denim, may be better suited for the projects presented in Chapter 3. Technically, they are stable enough for machine quilting, but the additional weight and bulk of the batting may not allow the garment to drape well, and it might not be comfortable for every climate or personal body thermostat. Loose-weave, limp, and light-weight fabrics such as blouse rayons, fine silks, sheers, or silky lining fabrics are not recommended. You will also want to avoid wools for this technique.

If you choose soft or medium- to light-weight fabrics, such as traditional quilters' cottons, light-weight chambray, linens, and various blends for your fabrics, be aware that they can develop ripples, puckers, and distortions when stitched. These fabrics cause fewer problems if they have been heavily starched first. You can spray starch the fabric sections or, as a better environmental choice, dip them into a mixture made from powdered concentrate or a commercially prepared liquid starch. It is easier to starch cut sections than yardage.

I use clothespins to secure the fabric to a clothesline suspended over my laundry tub, which allows the excess starch to drip into the tub. Once the piece is dry, I press it flat. Air drying starched fabric is a must because fabric dried with an iron will display a "white dandruff" of starch particles that haven't been absorbed by the fabric. If you are in a big hurry, use a hair dryer.

To verify that the section has been properly stabilized for machine quilting, add batting to a small sample and do a little trial stitching of the design you have selected. If it is not to your liking, starch again or select a different fabric.

Some fabrics may appear to be adequately starched but lose their crispness after some sewing. A light misting of starch and a warm iron should correct the problem, but do not forget to test first to be sure the marked design lines do not disappear or permanently discolor. After the sewing has been completed, always wash the fabric sections to remove the starch and carefully press them before you continue with the project.

Try one of my favorite tricks to prevent fabric from shifting during machine quilting. Use a moderately warm iron to press the batting to the fabric (batting side up and covered by a pressing cloth). If the iron is too hot, the batting could melt. Take care that your markings are not adversely affected by the pressing.

To reduce bulk and retain the draping quality of selected fabrics, it is best to work with two layers only, with the fashion fabric on top and the batting underneath. There are times when this is not possible. For instance, when you are sewing sharp curves or loops, the batting might drag on the machine or you might find that some types of threads do not form accurate stitches, even with a straight stitch. These problems can be corrected by basting a fabric backing under the batting to help the bottom layer feed smoothly through the machine. Prewashed, pressed, 100-percent cotton muslin is a good choice, but since this layer will be hidden by a lining, any 100-percent cotton print from your stash will do.

You may think that starching or adding muslin to stabilize the fabric and elevate the performance of your machine is a lot of extra work, but it is far more efficient than constantly repositioning fabric held in a hoop. Fusible tear-away is a more costly alternative, and it is not very compatible with batting because of the heat required for fusing. Small pieces of paper can be used as stabilizers under isolated designs; however, attempting to sew with one large piece of paper under an entire rectangle of fabric can be annoying. This method creates a rigid fabric unit, making it difficult to keep the paper in place. For those times that paper can be used successfully, end rolls of wide blank newsprint are handy and can be cut into any size. Newspaper publishers sometimes sell them and they are fairly inexpensive. Though more expensive, the thin white paper used for doctors' examination tables can be used, too. It can be purchased at medical supply stores.

Consider substituting commercial tear-away stabilizers for the batting to reduce bulk in areas such as pockets, collars, or lapels, as was done for the Running Parallel jacket. Select a lightweight stabilizer to avoid distorting the stitches when the stabilizer is torn away.

Although it may seem confusing to have so many stabilizing options, be assured that once you have become acquainted with these various methods, you will soon be able to analyze the characteristics of your fashion fabric and easily recognize which technique to use. To begin, you may want to select a fabric and garment shape similar to the project sample and follow the stabilizing instructions provided. Experiment with other options as you become more comfortable. Also, please acquaint yourself with the Thread and Stitching Tips (at right) and adapt as many as the project merits.

I cannot stress enough the importance of making a sample test of your thread, needle, tension, and fabric choices. Adjust as needed!

Thread and Stitching Tips

The following guidelines should help solve problems before they begin and make your sewing time more enjoyable:

Test machine stitches on the edges of the prepared fabric sandwich to confirm machine settings, thread color, and thread behavior before stitching in the actual garment area.

To obtain the best performance from your machine, use the proper needle for your project. Embroidery needles work well for most rayon threads.

Metallics perform best when these delicate threads are used with needles made just for them. These needles have larger, elongated eyes and sharper points than regular sewing needles, and an indentation in the front of the needle, above the eye, helps to reduce thread wear. Machine quilting or jeans needles can be used for this type of sewing, too. The needle sizes most often used for this type of sewing are 80/12 and 90/14.

Some metallic threads can be affected by high iron temperatures, resulting in color changes or damage to the thread. Use caution when pressing.

Always begin your project with a new needle.

Use an even-feed (walking foot) for the best results.

If possible, use an open-toe embroidery foot for better visibility.

To prevent some common stitching problems, try using a specialty thread in the needle and lingerie thread in the bobbin. Because lingerie thread is stretchy, it will pull the top thread down and prevent the bobbin thread from showing on top of the fabric. This method seems to work in most machines without your having to adjust the tension settings. Thread sold as bobbin thread is another excellent option to consider. Because lingerie thread and bobbin thread are so fine, a lot of thread fits on the bobbin, which reduces the need to rewind as often.

If the thread is still breaking, or the bobbin thread is showing on top, here are some things you can try: Re-thread your machine, slow your sewing speed, reduce the top tension, check the bobbin tension, and use a silicone lubricant on the thread. Also check the position of the spool on your machine. Some threads, such as the Mylar varieties, perform best when the spool is placed in a vertical position.

Skipping the last thread guide at the top of the needle shank may help prevent decorative threads from shredding. Many metallic threads are manufactured around a nylon core. If the last thread guide is too tight, the outer material will wear and separate.

Variegated threads give the illusion of a more complicated design.

Consider a heavier-weight thread for a more pronounced stitch or use two spools of thread, with both threads through the eye of one needle. Use a size 90 or 100 needle, which provides a larger eye.

To make the design stand out, you can use a narrow zigzag stitch, which will be more visible than a straight stitch.

Metallic thread will be more visible when stitched with a longer stitch length.

Echo-quilting can be used to increase the color and texture of a design.

You can use pre-programmed machine stitches, or you can explore the capabilities of your computerized machine for programming your own stitch patterns.

Make a hoop with your hands and fingers to keep the fabric flat and taut as you sew.

Do as much continuous-line sewing as possible.

Use the needle-down feature on your machine to avoid gaps in the sewing line that occur most often when sewing curves or corners.

Lock the beginning and ending of each line of stitches by setting the stitch length near zero and stitching several very close stitches. If available, use your automatic tie-off function on the machine. These two methods are preferable to backstitching, which can look untidy.

If you experience difficulties securing a thread knot when working with a slippery decorative thread in the needle and lingerie thread in the bobbin, pull the threads to the back of the work and tie off. It is more work, but it is better than having the design look messy with untidy thread ends. It's best to avoid using clear seam sealants because they have a tendency to discolor the fabric.

Some designs, such as grids, can be stitched beyond the marked pattern lines so that no locking of stitches is necessary. The stitches will be locked when garment is assembled.

Tic-Tac Copper Thread

Designing and Sewing

1. Select a vest pattern. Avoid any that have a seam in the back.

2. Make a small test sandwich of your fabric, batting, and muslin and stitch a motif or two to determine whether your fabric and thread combination will be suitable. If not, experiment and adjust according to the information provided in Thread and Stitching Tips, pages 42–43.

3. Follow the instructions for designing on fabric, page 10, and the Stori Lines for the Tic-Tac Copper Thread pattern.

4. Baste each fabric sandwich together.

5. Test stitch in the margin of the fabric section to confirm machine settings and thread choices.

6. Stitch the motifs for each section.

7. If you plan to add beads, do it now. Refer to page 14 for general beading instructions.

8. Confirm design placement and re-mark each fabric section with your correct-size,

The stitched and beaded vest shown on pages 45–46 provides an excellent introduction to the methods covered in this chapter. To complete it in a shorter amount of time, omit the beads and consider adding more stitching. The sample is made with a mid- to heavy-weight, 100-percent cotton sheeting fabric (not a bed sheet), because it is closely woven and stands up well when the design requires stitching isolated motifs. Look for this 60-inch-wide fabric at a full-service fabric store. Although the vest for this project was stitched with a simple straight stitch, it was necessary to add muslin under the batting to make the metallic thread behave properly. The lining is a 100-percent cotton batik. Narrow corded piping was incorporated, not only to provide a tidy edge, but also to complement the color of the thread and beads.

see-through patterns. Stay-stitch just outside the seam line around each shape to secure the batting. Cut out all the garment pieces.

9. Follow your pattern manufacturer's instructions for assembling the garment. To reduce bulk, trim the batting from all the seam allowances and press the allowances open.

10. Complete by lining the vest.

Photo 23: Tic-Tac Copper Thread vest (back view).

Tic-Tac Copper Thread Stori Lines

Unless the garment is very fitted, trace the correct-size pattern for this design.

Mark the tic-tac-toe designs onto each fabric section, referring to the pattern layout provided on page 47. Duplicates can be created by tracing the motifs from the book, or if you prefer, just eyeball these shapes as you draw. Keep them at least one inch away from the seam allowances. The edge of a see-through ruler will help to maintain straight parallel lines. Do not hesitate to rearrange the motifs to fit your garment.

The lengths of the lines and sizes of the motifs are purposely uneven.

Thread a machine embroidery needle with Mylar thread, positioning the spool so it feeds off a vertical spindle. Run a bead or two of silicone lubricant on the thread to reduce breakage. Use a lightweight thread in the bobbin, such as a bobbin or lingerie thread.

Check to be sure all the threads are secure after completing each section. Pull any loose threads to the back and tie off, if necessary.

Sew with a slightly longer than normal straight stitch, about 3.0mm to 3.5mm in length. (The stitch settings on most machine settings, especially those made overseas, are calibrated in millimeters.)

Add more stitching if beading is not planned.

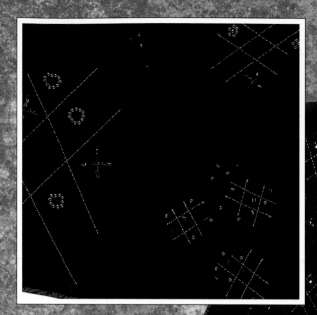

Photo 24: Tic-Tac Copper Thread vest (and detail), made by the author, was machine quilted with a straight stitch and Mylar thread. The vest was hand beaded with a variety of copper beads.

Stori Line Creations
Tic-Tac Copper Thread

Mix and match the designs on pages 87–88, or draw your own tic-tacs to fit your garment.

Running Parallel

The loose-fitting, shawl-collar jacket on the next page is punctuated with parallel lines, which are machine quilted through a stable, medium-weight, 100-percent cotton chambray. To provide a greater opportunity to coordinate the jacket with existing clothing in your wardrobe, the lines can be sewn with a variety of solid-color threads. A variegated thread may offer similar flexibility. A bright cotton print fabric was used to line the garment's body, while a silky rayon was used in the sleeves. To avoid excess bulk, the batting was eliminated in the pockets and collar facing.

Designing and Sewing

1. Select a jacket pattern. Look for one that does not require a seam in the back.

2. Using the stabilizing information in this chapter's introduction, make a small test fabric and batting sandwich and stitch a portion of this design. The cotton chambray jacket you see pictured was stabilized with batting alone; however, the addition of paper under the batting allows the stitches to form more evenly.

3. Follow the instructions for designing on fabric, page 10, and the Stori Lines for the Running Parallel pattern, page 52.

4. Baste the fabric and batting sandwiches for each garment section, except the reserved pieces, with small safety pins.

5. By practice-stitching several lines in the margin of your fabric section, you will become familiar with the settings of your particular machine and be able to sew attractive graduated parallel lines.

6. Repeat for all the fabric sandwiches.

7. Mark the desired parallel lines on the reserved pockets, collar, and lapel sections. To

reduce the bulk in these relatively small areas, use a tear-away stabilizer rather than batting. Before sewing the lines as described, test stitch in a margin and adjust the settings, if necessary. Remember, because these areas will not have batting, the machine set-up may differ.

8. Remove any paper or stabilizers from the wrong side of all fabric sections. Check to be sure all thread ends are securely knotted. If not, take the trouble to pull any loose ones to the wrong side and tie them so they do not migrate to the front of the jacket.

9. Confirm design placement and use your correct-size, see-through patterns to re-mark

the pattern size on each fabric section. Stay-stitch around each shape, just outside the seam line, to contain the batting. Cut out all the garment pieces.

10. Assemble the garment, following the pattern manufacturer's instructions. To reduce bulk, trim the batting from all the allowances and press them open.

11. Try on the jacket and study the design before lining it. If you think the piece would benefit by adding a few more lines, especially to balance the color, this is the time to do it.

12. Complete the jacket and enjoy!

Photo 25: Running Parallel jacket (back view).

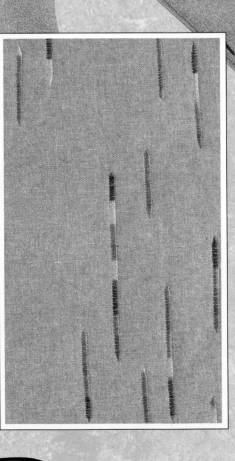

Photo 26: Running Parallel jacket, made by the author, was machine quilted with a zigzag stitch and rayon thread. In the detail at right, variegated thread has been used for variety.

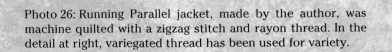

Stori Line Creations
Running Parallel

Draw parallel lines as desired to fit your garment pattern.

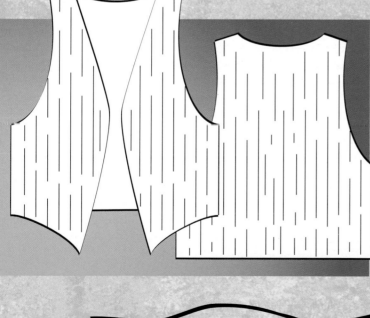

Running Parallel Stori Lines

Unless your garment pattern is very fitted, trace the correct size for this design. If your garment has pockets, a collar, or lapels, cut fabric sections for each, allowing about a one-inch margin around these smaller pieces. Mark their pattern outlines and retain these pieces to be used in Step 7.

Mark the parallel design lines directly onto the fabric. Because these are simple straight lines, no motifs were printed for this pattern. The lines on the jacket pictured varied in length from one to five inches. Keep the lines at least one inch away from the seam. To achieve lines that are vertical and straight, take special care to mark these lines parallel to the fabric's grain line as shown on your garment pattern. Refer to the project layout for suggested placement but arrange them wherever it makes sense for your pattern.

After marking one line, use a see-through ruler to measure and mark the additional randomly placed lines, measuring to the right and left of each line as desired. Varying the lengths of the lines will provide more visual interest.

It is a good idea to start marking a section that will be less noticeable, such as a sleeve. Mark it and continue with the next few steps with that one piece so that any design changes in placement, stabilizing, or color can be adjusted before continuing.

Thread a machine embroidery needle with 40-weight rayon thread and use a lightweight thread in the bobbin. An experiment with a heavier 30-weight embroidery thread in the needle revealed that the over-all appearance of the garment was better when the parallel lines had a slightly softer look. If a bolder look is what you want, go for it.

Set the machine to a zigzag stitch. The stitch length should be fairly close but not quite as close as a satin stitch. (Even with the aid of batting as a stabilizer, the chambray fabric began to tunnel and distort when the stitches were too dense.) Also the sample stitching performed better when paper was placed under the batting.

Adjust your stitch length to about .35 or .40 and the width to zero. Begin sewing by locking the threads, then immediately begin increasing the width of the stitch, sewing several stitches at each setting until you reach the desired width. Sew at that width until you are almost at the end of the marked line. Then decrease the width as evenly as possible, ending with a zero stitch width and lock the stitches.

Although it is more time consuming, the color placement is easier to control by working on one fabric section at a time. The darkest color was selected first, and various marked lines on that section were randomly stitched. The process was repeated until all the colors had been used.

Try to do a little planning as you stitch so that when you are sewing the final color, red for instance, all the red lines are not next to each other.

Do not worry about following each of the lines exactly as you have marked them. The colors of your threads may help dictate the final decision regarding the location and length of your design.

After the piece was half sewn, the chambray was beginning to soften and pucker slightly from handling. A light misting of spray starch and a warm iron provided just enough stiffness to keep the fabric smooth during the final stitching. This action did not produce any stains on the fabric, but be sure to test your marking tools before resorting to this interim stabilizing procedure.

Thank You Debra and Michael

The free-flowing streamers featured on the wholecloth dress shown on page 56 were created to complement the pleated skirt. The variegated rayon thread draws the eye down to alternating strips of black, 100-percent cotton fabric and the gradations of Debra Lunn and Michael Mrowka's Pointillist Palette© collection. Small circular stitches provide additional interest and act like tacking stitches to help hold the batting in place.

Designing and Sewing

1. Select a garment pattern. If you are unable to find a dress pattern with a pleated skirt, look for one with a loose-fitting bodice and use the following method to adapt it to make the pleats:

Measure around the bottom edge of the bodice pattern pieces (minus seam allowances and center front overlap) to obtain the finished measurement. Multiply that figure by three to obtain the approximate measurement around the top edge of the skirt before pleating.

Notice that the skirt is made of several pairs of vertical strips. (A pleated pair consists of a black strip and a colored one.) To determine how many pairs you need to sew, divide the number of inches you need for the top edge of the skirt by the finished width of the pair. For instance, if the finished colored strip is 1½" and the finished black strip is 3½" wide. The finished width of the pair is 5". If the bodice measurement is 25", three times 25 equals 75". Then 75" divided by 5" equals 15 pairs of strips for the skirt.

To cut the strips, be sure to add ½" to the width of each strip for seam allowances. Also keep in mind that, when pleated, the top of the skirt must be the same diameter as the bottom edge of the bodice. You may find that a few strips need to be a little wider or narrower to make everything fit.

To assemble the skirt, use a ¼" seam allowance to strip piece the cut fabric strips together. Starting with a black strip, alternate the black strips with the colored ones.

Pressing the skirt to form the pleats is easier to accomplish before the final seam has been sewn. Working from the top edge of the skirt and from left to right, fold a colored strip underneath the adjacent black strip and press. Secure the pleat with straight pins. Repeat for the remaining pleats. Looking at the right side of the skirt, you will see only the black strips. Thread baste (removing the pins as you go) down from the top edge of the skirt for 3" along the edge of each pleat.

Before sewing the last two strips together, which joins the strips in a circle, measure the top edge of the skirt (minus the seam allowances for the final seam). Compare this measurement with the measurement for the bottom of the bodice and adjust the width of the last seam allowance, if necessary, so the skirt will fit the bodice. When you are satisfied that the finished diameter will fit the bodice properly, sew the final vertical skirt seam, and press and pin the last pleat. Sew the pleated skirt to the bodice and press again.

Use the same weight of 100-percent cotton fabric for the bodice and pleated skirt sections. A good quality medium-weight traditional quilters' cotton is best. It may be easier to select the multi-colored fabric sections for the skirt before choosing the main color of the dress, since those options may be sparser. Strips can be cut from gradations of hand-dyed fabrics, or you can consider using one big print cut into strips.

Do some preplanning so that the appropriate amount of fabric can be purchased. What fabric will you use for lining? Do you want to add coordinating cuffs or a collar?

2. Follow the instructions for designing on fabric, page 10, and the Stori Lines for the Thank You Debra and Michael pattern, page 55.

3. Because of the loop-the-loop stitching, you will need to work with a sandwich of fabric, batting, and muslin. For best results, tape the muslin to a work table, cover it with the batting, then the cotton fabric, marked side up. Generously pin baste with small safety pins.

4. Practice stitching some streamers in the margin of your fabric section until you become familiar with the settings of your particular machine.

Even though this is not free-motion sewing and, hopefully, your machine will be equipped with a walking foot, you will need to move the fabric sections as if the feed dogs were lowered. Remember to use your hands like a hoop to keep the fabric taut as you sew.

Areas free of streamers will require some sort of tacking stitches to hold the batting in position. If your machine has an eyelet stitch, program it to stitch a single one. Again, test the eyelet in the margin before committing to the garment. Stitch the eyelets one at a time, scattering them evenly throughout the garment. An alternative might be a tailor's tack, or even a ½" length of concentrated zigzag stitches.

6. Confirm design placement and re-mark each fabric section with your correct-size, see-through patterns. Stay-stitch around each shape, just outside the seam line to secure the batting. Cut out the garment.

7. Sew the pleated skirt following the instructions in Step 1.

8. Follow the pattern manufacturer's instructions for assembling the garment. To reduce bulk, trim the batting from the seam allowances where possible and press them open.

Thank You Debra and Michael Stori Lines

Trace only the bodice and sleeve pattern pieces onto the rectangular or square fabric sections.

Mark the streamer lines by drawing free-hand, similar to the motif provided. Use the grain lines on your pattern piece to help guide the placement of the streamers so they will be fairly vertical. There is no magic formula for drawing these flowing lines, but try to maintain curvy lines rather than angular ones. Draw as many or as few as appropriate for your figure and dress pattern. If you are large, pay special attention to the placement over the breast area. Feel free to mark and sew only a few major lines at first and then add more as the design develops. The colors of the thread may impact how many lines you want. Do not be afraid to follow your instincts.

Thread a machine embroidery needle with 40-weight rayon variegated thread and use a lightweight thread in the bobbin.

Start stitching the streamers at least one inch outside the outline of the garment. It is not necessary to lock these stitches. That will be accomplished when the garment is constructed.

A narrow, fairly open zigzag will look best and be the easiest to stitch. Begin each line with a .40 length and 1.5 width, gradually reducing the length and width at the end of each streamer until you are stitching nearly in place several times to lock the threads. This technique produces visually pleasing streamers by eliminating abrupt bluntly stitched ends.

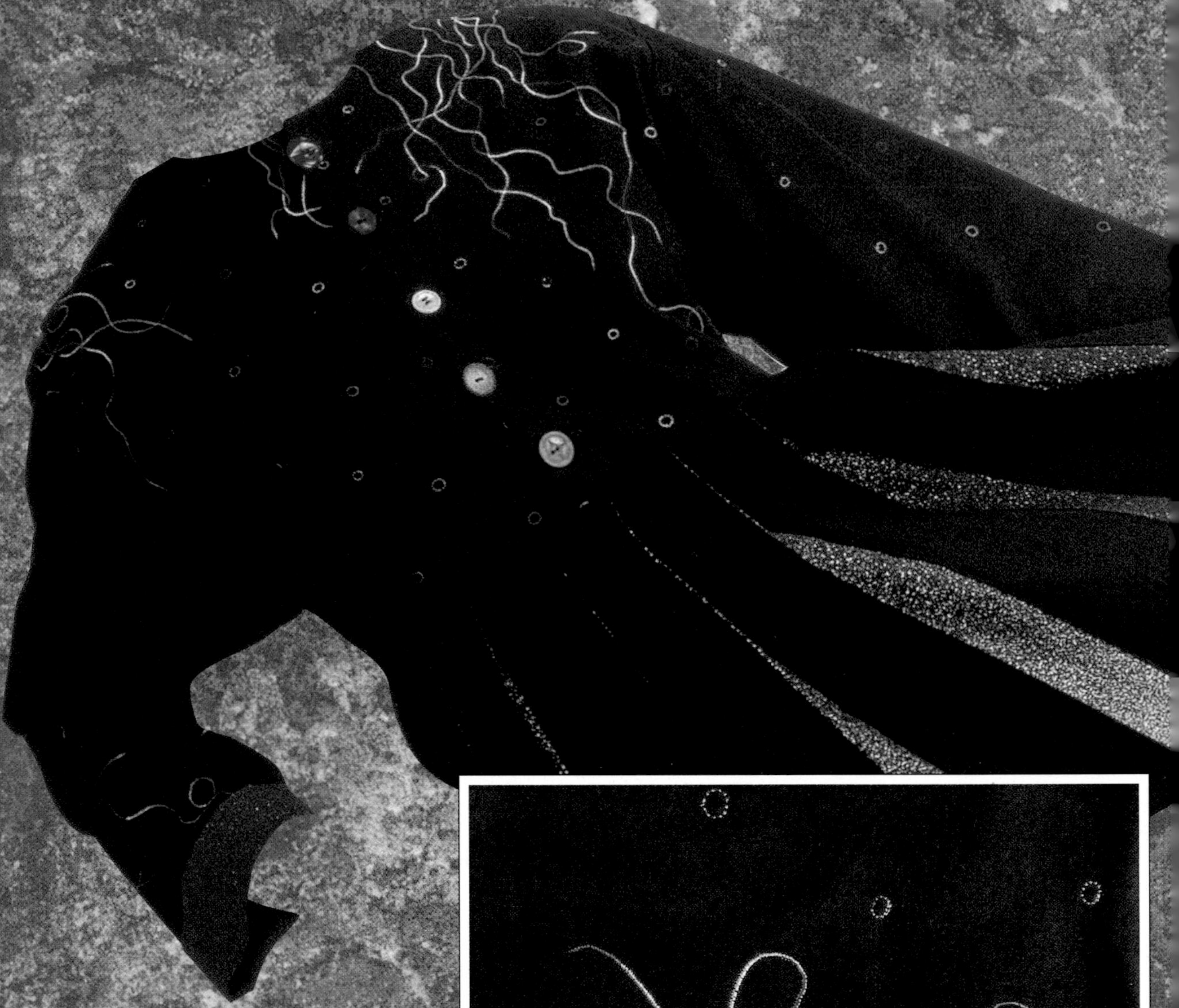

Photo 27: Thank You Debra and Michael dress, made by the author. The pleated skirt features fabric from the Pointillist Palette Collection by Debra Lunn and Michael Mrowka.

Photo 28: Thank You Debra and Michael (detail) was machine quilted with a variegated thread in a zigzag stitch and an eyelet. The feed dogs were engaged during sewing.

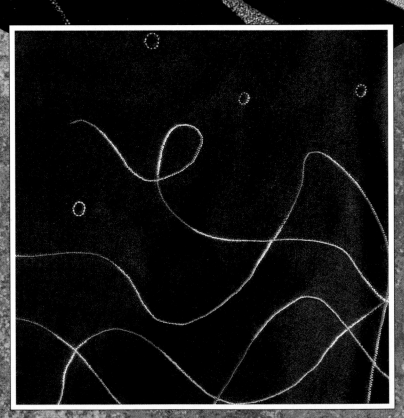

Stori Line Creations

Thank You
Debra and Michael

Mix and match the patterns on pages 89–90, or draw your own streamers to fit your garment.

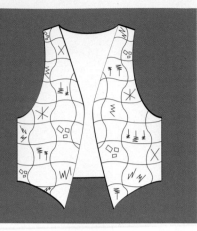

Always Wavering

Because of the rather lightweight, floppy nature of the fabric used in the jumper shown in Photo 29, stabilizing each fabric section with starch became necessary. To provide a bolder overall look to the design, the stitching was accomplished by sewing with two strands of thread in the needle. Because of the homespun nature of the fabrics, cotton-covered polyester threads were used rather than decorative ones.

This jumper was inspired by a coarsely woven strip fabric that had been in my collection for ages. The colors never seemed to work with any ongoing projects until I came across a solid-green cotton and linen blend. It was not only the perfect color match for the bodice, but the correct look and feel.

Designing and Sewing

1. Select a jumper pattern.

2. Stabilize your fabric by starching according to the information provided in this chapter's introduction. Be sure that very drapey fabrics are stiffly starched.

3. Follow the directions for designing on paper, page 8, and the Stori Lines for the Always Wavering pattern.

4. Baste the marked starched fabric sections and batting together with small safety pins.

5. Test stitch in the margin of one of the bodice sections to obtain the correct machine settings and thread choices, then sew the designs.

6. Remove any paper from the wrong side of the fabric sections. Check to be sure that all thread ends are securely knotted.

7. Confirm the design placement and mark the correct-size, see-through pattern on each fabric section. Stay-stitching is not mandatory for this jumper bodice because the batting is fairly well secured by the wavy lines. Cut out the garment.

8. Assemble the jumper, following the pattern manufacturer's instructions. To reduce bulk, trim the batting from the seam allowances and press allowances open. Line the bodice and complete with binding if desired.

Fig. 9. Stop sewing approximately 2" short of the seam line.

Fig. 10. Draw a line to connect the two wavy lines at the seam. Finish sewing the wavy line across the seam.

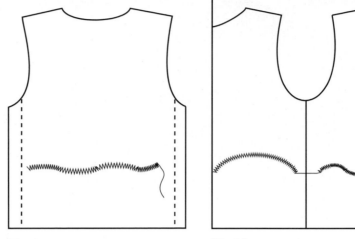

Fig. 9   Fig. 10

Always Wavering Stori Lines

Mark a vertical center line on each paper bodice section. Place small reference marks in one-inch increments on either side of the center line at the top and bottom of the marked garment outline. Examine the spacing and decide how many motifs will best suit your garment. Use these marks as guides and draw as many wavy lines as needed from top to bottom. Repeat the procedure to create the horizontal wavy lines. Keep in mind that, in some areas, the spaces may be as far apart as two inches.

Trace the individual motifs provided onto the paper pattern in a pleasing arrangement within the sections created by the wavy lines. Do not be afraid to vary and play with the layout provided until it suits you. Retrace the final paper pattern to your starched fabric.

Position two spools of conventional cotton-covered polyester thread on the spindles of your machine. Treat the threads as one, passing them together through the eye of a machine embroidery needle (size 90/14). Use a lightweight thread in the bobbin. If you prefer a softer look, use only one spool of thread.

Set the machine to a zigzag stitch. You will be sewing all the wavy lines first. The stitch length should be fairly close, such as a .40 length combined with a 2.0 width, but not quite as close as a satin stitch. Keep the fabric taut with your fingers as you sew.

Sew the grid first. Begin and end the long wavy lines about one inch beyond the marked garment shape at the neckline and bottom edge. This allows the stitching to be secured when the garment is constructed.

Here is a foolproof way to ensure that the wavy lines meet perfectly at the seams. Begin and end these wavy lines of stitching about two inches short of the shoulder and side seams (Fig. 9). Cut the thread tails long, pull them to the back, and tie them off. After the seam has been sewn during garment assembly, mark a connecting line across the seam between the two wavy lines. Stitch the connecting line and again leave long thread tails. Pull the thread ends to back and tie them off (Fig. 10). If you prefer, instead of matching the wavy lines at the seam, you can draw them so that they purposely don't meet. Be sure they are far enough apart so that it doesn't look like you tried but missed.

After all the wavy lines have been sewn, set the stitches for the inside motifs at .40 long and 1.5 wide. For sewing these concentrated designs, the fabric sections will slide through the machine much better when paper is placed under the area being sewn.

Photo 29. Always Wavering jumper (back view) was machine quilted with two strands of thread in the needle to provide a bolder stitch. The cotton and linen lightweight fabric was stabilized with starch.

The Wholecloth Garment Stori

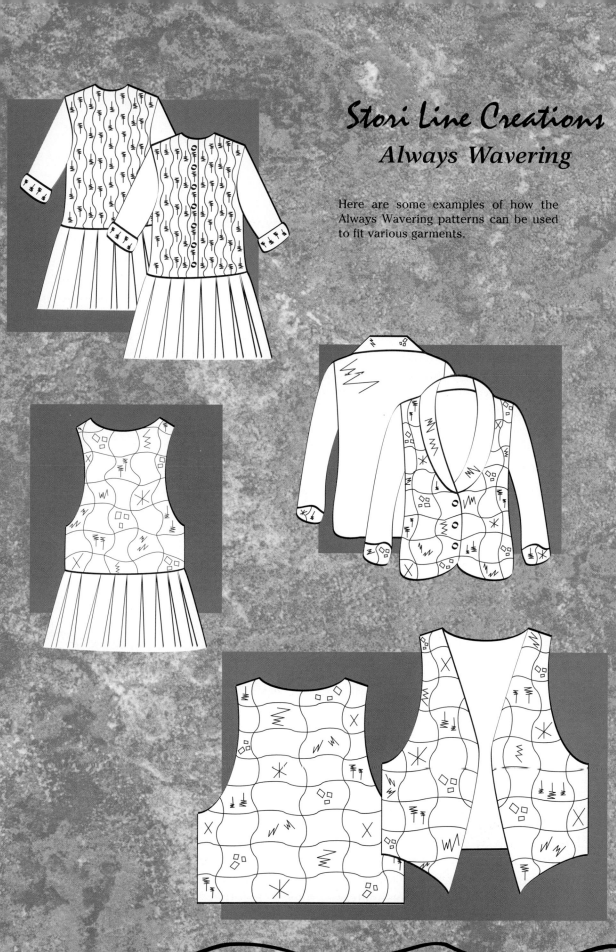

Stori Line Creations
Always Wavering

Here are some examples of how the Always Wavering patterns can be used to fit various garments.

Chapter 3

Machine Embroidery

There is nothing fancy about the version of machine embroidery presented in this chapter. All you need is a simple zigzag stitch. The batting that was used to stabilize the fabric in Chapter 2 is absent. Typically, machine embroidery is accomplished with the fabric secured in a hoop. The technique described in this chapter eliminates that requirement. It also avoids the necessity of sewing with the somewhat expensive water-soluble stabilizers and the uncertain effect tear-away products may have on your designs. You will find that the stabilizing approach introduced in this chapter is fast and easy, and it is one that can be applied to many of the designs in the first two chapters.

The following projects will be beneficial for sewers in warmer climates and those who prefer light-weight clothing. To provide additional ideas, some of the designs were created to complement a print fabric in the ensemble or lining, a technique you can use to add versatility to your wardrobe. Please become familiar with the following guidelines and, before beginning a project, thoroughly read its instructions.

Stabilizing Method

Fusible-tricot interfacing is the key ingredient (Photo 30). This product was originally designed to be used with knit fabrics. The fiber content varies from one manufacturer to another. Generally you will find 100-percent nylon or 100-percent polyester. Unfortunately, this interfacing is readily available in only narrow widths, such as 20 or 24 inches. Some mail-order sources offer it in 60-inch widths, which is a better buy. Many fusible interfacings require preshrinking before use. It is slightly troublesome but not as annoying or damaging as having your fabric bubble after fusing. Dedicated sewers may want to purchase this interfacing by the bolt and preshrink the whole amount so it is always ready to use.

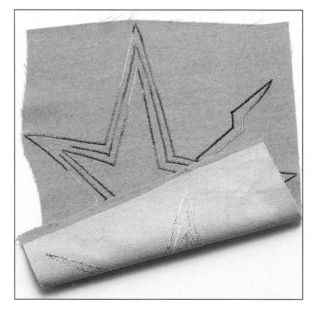

Photo 30: Sample: Silk noil stabilized with light-weight, drapeable, fusible-tricot interfacing.

The process of stabilizing fabric with this product is simple. Cut only the amount you need. It is not necessary to cover every square inch of your fabric section. Just be sure there is a sufficient amount of interfacing behind your pattern piece. If a wider amount is needed, like for the back of a garment, butting two pieces together is acceptable. To ensure an invisible seam in the interfacing, carefully trim edges with a rotary cutter before butting them together. Center the interfacing, rough adhesive side toward the wrong side of the fabric section, and fuse them together, following the manufacturer's instructions. Please note that fusing instructions can differ depending on the company.

One new toy that I have in my sewing room, which makes fast work of this procedure, is a professional ironing system for household use. Steam (and there is a ton of it) is generated in a separate water tank. Suction holds the fabric in place on the ironing board and draws the steam right through it.

It is important to get a good bond when fusing the interfacing. Steam and heat act together to melt the glue, which is the bonding agent, to ensure a permanent, bubble-free application. Once the section has been fused, mark the outline of the garment pattern on the right side of the fabric section and proceed as directed in the instructions for the project you have selected. Take time to test the interfacing on your fabric before beginning any project. Disappointments are best faced at this stage.

Fabric Suggestions

Freedom of choice and quick results are the chief benefits of this stabilizing technique. You will find that fabrics backed with a fusible interfacing become considerably more stable, allowing a greater spectrum of fabrics to be considered. How the fabric behaves during stitching is not the only thing to consider. The weight and fiber content also ultimately affect how the garment looks on the body. Remember, stitching always add stiffness, so

the goal is to achieve yardage that is drapeable, yet pucker-free. Naturally, test your selection to be sure it is suitable before committing to a plan. It's a good idea to wash and dry all fabrics before fusing to prevent problems that can occur if the fabric shrinks during the bonding process. For some fabrics, such as wool, washing is not possible. Testing these fabrics is imperative.

Most woven fabrics can be used successfully with this technique, including medium- to heavy-weight cottons; medium- to heavy-weight silks; silk noil; linens and linen blends; wool and wool blends; and sturdier rayons, challis, and acrylics. In most cases, the addition of the interfacing allows distortion-free stitching without a hoop. Feel free to experiment with fabrics not mentioned.

For wholecloth garments, it's best to exclude extremely heavy denims, canvas, and upholstery fabrics, which are generally too stiff when combined with a permanently fused backing and concentrated stitching. Avoid loosely woven, light-weight fabrics, such as blouse rayons, fine silks, sheers, and silky lining fabrics. Also avoid sweatshirt fleece or knits because the appearance and drape of these fabrics combined with fused interfacing is generally not attractive. However, if a specific fabric of this nature really inspires your creativity, do not hesitate to experiment before dismissing its possibilities. Also experiment first when using fabrics with a nap because fusing may affect the appearance of the fabric. It might be just the perfect background for your design. Just be sure to test it first.

Zigzag Stitching

The following hints and illustrations show you how to sew curves and corners with the zigzag stitch. Be sure to review the Thread and Stitching Tips offered in Chapter 2 (pages 42–43) because many of them will be applicable to this chapter. TEST, TEST, TEST your machine settings and thread choices in the margins of your fabric sections before starting on a garment.

Photo 31: Positive/Negative (detail). Narrow zigzag stitching enhances this geometric design.

When machine embroidering these garments, the thing to remember is to secure with a straight stitch; embroider with a zigzag. Use the straight stitch first to further stabilize the fabric and provide a guide for sewing evenly spaced zigzag stitches.

Set the machine for a straight stitch that is slightly shorter than the normal stitch length (about 2.0). Start by straight stitching at the beginning of one of the lines or motifs. Stop sewing with the needle down at the end of the line. Raise the presser foot, and reposition the fabric so you will be sewing toward the direction you began. Lower the presser foot. Change the machine setting to the appropriate zigzag length and width. You want a slightly open stitch, not quite a satin stitch. Check the needle position and adjust the fabric, if necessary, so that the straight stitch is in the center of the zigzag stitch. Sew to the starting point. Pull threads to the back and tie off or use the automatic tie-off function on your machine.

Turning Corners

To achieve crisp corners when zigzag stitching, stitch until the needle is just past the corner. For outside corners, stop the machine with the needle in the fabric on the outside edge of the zigzag. Raise the presser foot, pivot the fabric, lower the presser foot, and continue stitching, overlapping the right angle corner (Fig. 11). For inside corners, stop the machine with the needle in the fabric on the inside of the zigzag stitch. Raise the presser foot, pivot the fabric, lower presser foot, and continue stitching (Fig. 12). There may be times you will have to adjust the position of the fabric slightly to compensate for the stitch width when you turn the corner.

Sewing Curves

To avoid gaps when stitching curves, allow the feed dogs and walking foot to work for you. Take your time. Do not push the fabric through the machine too quickly. From time to time, you will need to stop with the needle in the down position and pivot to reposition the fabric. The wider the stitch and the tighter the curve, the more often you will need to pivot. To sew outside curves, stop with needle down on the outside swing, then pivot (Fig. 13). For inside curves, stop with the needle down on the inside swing, then pivot (Fig. 14).

Creating Sharp Points

Some designs require sewing points rather than squared corners, such as the tips of stars or the jagged edges of lightning bolts. Stitch with the appropriate zigzag setting until you are about one inch from the point, or for smaller designs, you may want to be even closer to the point. From there, gradually but steadily decrease the stitch width as you sew to narrow the point. At the end of thc point, you should be on or near zero. Stop with the needle down, then pivot. Stitch slowly, increasing the stitch width for about an inch, or less for smaller designs, until you reach your original setting (Fig. 15).

Construction Tips

If the fabric section becomes too limp or starts to ripple slightly, a light pressing usually restores crispness. For additional firmness, you can use a little spray starch. Be sure your design markings will not fade or stain the fabric before you attempt to press the fabric.

Press seam allowances open to reduce the slight bulk created by the interfacing. Be careful not to use an iron that is too hot. In some cases, the heat can loosen the interfacing and melt or discolor some decorative threads.

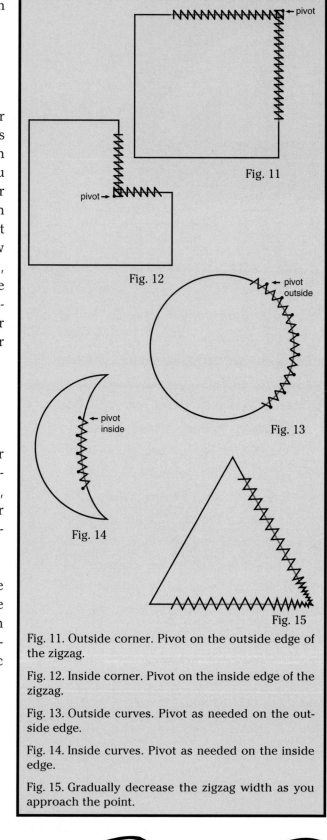

Fig. 11. Outside corner. Pivot on the outside edge of the zigzag.

Fig. 12. Inside corner. Pivot on the inside edge of the zigzag.

Fig. 13. Outside curves. Pivot as needed on the outside edge.

Fig. 14. Inside curves. Pivot as needed on the inside edge.

Fig. 15. Gradually decrease the zigzag width as you approach the point.

Mad for Plaid

The inspiration for this project came from a madras plaid found on a sale table. The fabric was a fitting companion for the jacket's coarsely woven blue hemp fabric, which looks and feels like a nubby linen. The easy-to-stitch designs featured on the jacket present a wearable yet distinctive garment that can be completed quickly. Sewing with variegated rayon thread allows the motifs to appear more complex than they are while repeating the color scheme. Stabilizing is achieved with fusible tricot interfacing, as described on page 62. The focus of this project is the jacket, but ambitious readers may want to create a complete ensemble similar to the one pictured in Photo 32.

Designing and Sewing

1. Select any garment pattern that you like.

2. Cut fabric sections for each major pattern piece and apply a knit fusible interfacing according to the manufacturer's directions.

3. Follow the instructions for designing on fabric, page 10, and the Stori Lines for the Mad for Plaid pattern on the facing page.

4. Test stitch a portion of the design in the margin of a fabric section. Make appropriate machine and thread adjustments. Stitch the designs.

5. If you find the fabric is slightly out of shape, press it lightly so that you will be working with a flat piece for the next step. Check again to be sure all thread ends are secure.

6. Confirm the design placement and re-mark the pattern size on each fabric section with your correct-size, see-through patterns. Cut out the garment.

7. Assemble the garment, following the pattern manufacturer's instructions. A coordinating print lining fabric and binding will complete your jacket.

Photo 32: Whitney Schroeder models the Mad for Plaid jacket, made by the author. The variegated thread used to sew the lopsided designs echoes the colors of the madras plaid fabric.

Mad for Plaid Stori Lines

Unless your garment pattern is fitted or you plan to stitch considerably more designs onto the fabric than shown in the layout, trace using your correct size.

The motifs can be drawn directly onto the fabric free-hand or with the aid of a small ruler and your favorite marking tool. If it makes you feel more confident, trace the motifs onto pieces of white paper, place them in the desired location under your fabric, and use a light box to retrace them on the fabric. Naturally, if marking directly on the fabric makes you cringe, use the instructions for designing on a paper pattern first.

Remember, this is not rocket science. Place the motifs wherever it makes sense for your specific garment. Consider using just one of the motifs from the overlapped compositions to increase the design options, or you can draw more yourself. The designs were purposely created to be uneven and lopsided and to provide a variety of sizes, which keeps the overall impact from being dull.

Equip your machine with an embroidery needle (90/14) and thread it with a 40-weight rayon, variegated thread or a thread of your choice. Use a lightweight thread in the bobbin.

Set the machine for a straight stitch (about 2.0). Begin at one end of the motif and straight stitch the entire design, pivot, and switch to the desired zigzag setting (about .35 long and 1.5 wide), and sew back to the starting point. Refer to the general embroidery instructions, page 65.

Continue stitching in this manner until all the motifs on each fabric section have been sewn. Be sure to secure or tie off all thread ends.

Photo 33: Mad For Plaid jacket (back view). The stabilized hemp fabric permits the narrow zigzag designs to be stitched pucker-free.

The Wholecloth Garment Stori

Stori Line Creations
Mad for Plaid

Here are some examples of how the Mad for Plaid patterns can be used to fit various garments.

Heat Lightning

In an effort to add variety to my wardrobe, I made the dress on page 72 with yellow silk noil for the bodice and a coordinating crinkled cotton print fabric for the skirt, collar, and cuffs. The colors of the print fabric were easily duplicated for the motifs by sewing with rayon variegated threads. My design objective was to achieve a subtle look; therefore, I purposely chose to stitch with a very narrow zigzag, which kept the designs from becoming too bold.

Since decorative stitching is applied to only the main bodice sections, stabilizing was required for just those pattern pieces. The motifs are slightly more complex but still quite easy to sew. Feel free to make your garment with one solid-color fabric or solid-color thread, if you prefer.

Designing and Sewing

1. Select your favorite dress pattern.

2. Cut fabric sections for the major bodice pattern pieces only and apply a knit fusible interfacing according to the pattern manufacturer's directions. Retain other pattern pieces and use them as you normally would during the construction of the garment.

3. Follow the instructions for designing on fabric, page 10, and the Stori Lines for the Heat Lightning pattern. Be sure to test stitch a generous portion of one of the designs in the margin of a fabric section. Make appropriate machine and thread adjustments as needed.

4. If you find that the fabric is getting slightly out of shape as you stitch the designs, press it lightly so that you will have a flat piece of fabric for the next step. Check again to be sure all thread ends are securely knotted.

5. Confirm the design placement and mark the correct-size, see-through pattern on each fabric section. Cut out the garment pieces.

6. Follow the pattern manufacturer's instructions for assembling the garment.

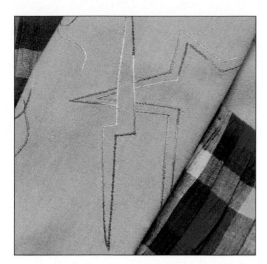

Photo 34: Heat Lightning (detail). Plan the stitching order for those designs that over-lap. You can use the edge of the presser foot as a guide to echo-embroider the stars.

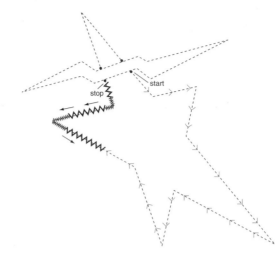

Fig. 16: For overlapping motifs, sew the one underneath first. Lock or tie-off the threads at the starting and stopping points.

Heat Lightning Stori Lines

Unless your garment pattern is fitted, use your correct size for tracing.

Trace each motif several times (which will provide more patterns to play with) onto freezer paper or template material and cut them out. Referring to the design layout for placement ideas, arrange the shapes within the boundaries of your marked fabric section. Alter the placement any way that is flattering. Don't forget to consider turning the designs over (mirror image) or turning them in any direction to increase your design options. Designing in this manner is simpler if you tackle one section at a time.

Echo embroidery lines for the stars can be drawn directly on the fabric. Use a small ruler to keep the lines even. If you prefer, you can stitch the echo lines without marking them first by using the edge of your presser foot as a guide.

Equip your machine with an embroidery needle (90/14) and use a 40-weight variegated, rayon thread. You may want to use contrasting colors of thread to allow the different designs to be discernible. Try blues for the lightning bolts, and perhaps, reds, yellows, and pinks for the stars. Use a lightweight thread in the bobbin.

Examine your layout to determine a logical order for sewing the motifs. Start by stitching those that lie under other designs. Take a moment to study Fig. 16, which shows the sewing order for overlapping motifs. Sew from "start" to "stop" with a straight stitch. Stop with the needle down. Pivot the fabric and switch to your desired zigzag setting (about .40 or .50 long and 1.5 wide). Sew back along the motif to where you began, covering the straight stitches with the zigzags. Lock or tie the threads. Repeat for the portion of the motif on the other side of the overlapping design.

When stitching isolated motifs, start sewing in the middle of one of the straight lines rather than at a point or corner.

Continue sewing until you have stitched all the motifs with one thread color before switching to another color. Tie off or lock any stitches that will not be covered by another line of sewing.

Photo 35: Heat Lightning dress (back view). Stabilizing expands your fabric options. The silk noil fabric features designs created with variegated threads, which help to create a sense of depth as the colors fade in and out.

Stori Line Creations
Heat Lightning

Here are some examples of how the Heat Lightning patterns can be used to fit various garments.

Positive/ Negative

A comfortable, casual pullover shirt is a welcome addition to anyone's wardrobe. The notion of using sweatshirt fleece for this garment was dismissed because of the stretchy nature of the fabric. Instead, the shirt was made with a medium-weight, fairly sturdy 100-percent cotton woven fabric. The tricot fusible interfacing guaranteed the necessary stability for the concentrated stitching, yet the draping quality one expects of this type of garment was not compromised. To achieve as much visual impact as possible and still keep the lines narrow, a heavier 30-weight rayon embroidery thread was used for the stitching. The shirt was lined with a thin cotton flannel for added comfort.

Designing and Sewing

1. Select a pullover pattern. (The pattern used was Stretch and Sew #341, View A).

2. Cut fabric sections for each major pattern piece and apply a knit fusible interfacing according to the manufacturer's directions.

3. Follow the method for designing on paper, page 8, and the Stori Lines for the Positive/ Negative pattern.

4. Test stitch a portion of one of the designs in the margin of a fabric section and make the appropriate machine and thread adjustments.

5. After all sections have been stitched, press lightly with steam so that you will be working with a flat piece of fabric for the next step. Again, check to be sure all thread ends are securely knotted.

6. Confirm design placement and use your correct-size, see-through pattern to re-mark the garment on each fabric section. Cut out the garment pieces.

7. Assemble the garment, following the pattern manufacturer's instructions. Add lining and ribbing to complete your pullover.

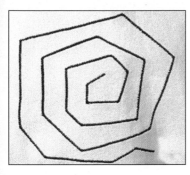

Photo 36

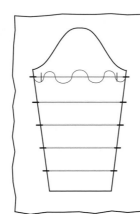

Fig. 17

Photo 36: Positive/Negative pullover (detail). Heavier 30-weight rayon thread produces more distinctive design lines.

Fig. 17: On your paper pattern, draw guide lines across the garment, between the marks, to help in placing the wavy lines.

Positive/Negative Stori Lines

Since these patterns are usually generously sized, you can use your correct size for designing and sewing.

Refer to the design layout and individual motifs to aid you in re-creating the design on your paper pattern. Do not be afraid to make changes. If you prefer to stitch only on the front of your shirt, it is perfectly okay. Or if you want to reduce the number of motifs, do so. Remember, you are in charge of the needle and thread.

When drawing the wavy lines on the paper sleeve pattern, use the following tip: Make small reference marks on one edge of a sleeve. Duplicate those marks on the opposite edge of the sleeve. Using a ruler, light-ly draw a straight line, connecting each set of marks (Fig. 17). Beginning 1½" in from the sleeve edge, start drawing a wavy line, using the straight line as a reference. These curves do not need to be exact. End the wavy line 1½" before the sleeve edge.

If your markings will not rub off too easily, trace the entire design onto the prepared fabric sections.

Because my soap sliver markings were a little difficult to see on the white fabric and because they rubbed off fairly quickly, I marked and sewed only a portion of the design at a time. Retracing was not a hassle because I was able to easily see the black design lines on my paper pattern through my white stabilized fab-ric without using a light box. Naturally, a light source may be required, depending on the fabric choice.

Equip your machine with an embroidery needle (90/14) and use a 30-weight solid-color embroidery thread. Variegated thread may not be a good choice because it blurs the design. Use a lightweight thread in the bobbin.

Examine your layout. You will want to sew all the short lines first so that overlapping lines can lock and hide where those stitches begin and end. Set the machine for a straight stitch (about 2.0).

Begin by straight stitching one of the short lines. At the end of the line, leaving the needle in the fabric, pivot the fabric and switch to your desired zigzag setting (about .40 or .50 long and 2.0 wide). Sew with the zigzag stitch back to the starting point, keeping the zigzag stitch centered on the straight stitch.

Continue stitching in this manner, alternating between sewing the short lines and the longer overlapped lines. Tie off or lock any stitches that will not be covered by another line of sewing. Stitch the motifs in the same way, re-marking them if necessary.

There is quite a bit of stitching on this garment. If the fabric becomes limp from handling, mist lightly with spray starch and press. Be sure to test the reaction of your marking tool first in the margin before using starch.

Photo 37: Positive/Negative pullover, made by the author. Do not limit your designs only to jackets and vests. Medium-weight stabilized cotton maintains the draping quality required for this style of garment.

Stori Line Creations
Positive/Negative

Here are some examples of how the Positive/Negative patterns can be used to fit various garments.

Twice As Nice

Cotton sheeting was used for the inside and the outside of this reversible vest pictured on page 80. To prevent the garment from becoming too stiff, only the side with the plaid design was fused with tricot interfacing. For the reverse side, the densely woven fabric was sufficiently sturdy to allow the sewing machine's computerized designs to be stitched with the aid of ordinary white notebook paper used as a stabilizer. If your machine is not equipped with programmed stitches, consider using a coordinating plaid fabric for the lining instead.

The following instructions assume that you will be making the vest reversible.

Designing and Sewing

1. Select a vest pattern. For ease in designing, select a loose-fitting vest with a one-piece back and no collar.

2. Cut fabric sections of medium-weight cotton sheeting for each major pattern piece. You will need to cut two rectangles for each front and one square for each back (a total of four rectangles and two squares). Following the pattern manufacturer's directions, apply knit fusible interfacing to the wrong side of one set of fabric sections (two rectangles and one square).

3. Follow the instructions for designing on paper, page 8, for the "plaid" side. The decorative stitching for the reverse side can be planned directly on the fabric. Be sure to review the Stori Lines on page 79 for additional helpful instructions and options for creating these designs.

4. Test stitch portions of all the designs in the margins of the appropriate fabric sections. Make any necessary machine and thread adjustments. Sew the designs using the hints in the Stori Lines.

5. After all sections have been stitched, press lightly so that you will be working with a flat

piece of fabric for the next step. Check to be sure all thread ends are securely knotted.

6. Confirm the design placement and re-mark each fabric section using your correct-size, see-through patterns for the reverse side. To ensure that the plaid lines will match up, re-mark these sections with the paper pattern you have designed, aligning the plaid lines properly before cutting the garment pieces out. The stitching lines that end in a seam allowance will be locked by the seam stitching. If an abnormal amount of shrinkage occurs, be sure to lengthen the plaid lines with additional stitching before cutting out the garment.

7. Assemble the garment following the pattern manufacturer's instructions.

Twice As Nice Stori Lines

Plaid Side

Make the paper pattern your correct size. Because both sides of the vest front are identical, you will need to draw only one side, then reverse the pattern for the second side. Refer to the Stori Line Creations on page 83, as you measure and draw the plaid lines onto your paper pattern. Check the grain line on your pattern and use it as a guide when marking the first vertical line to ensure correct placement. A see-through ruler will help you measure and maintain accuracy. The style and size of your garment may necessitate some design adjustments. Be sure to match the location of any vertical or horizontal lines that must meet at the side and shoulder seams. As a design option, consider placing the lines on the diagonal or using checks instead of plaids.

Once you are satisfied with the design, use a light box to trace the paper pattern to the fused fabric sections. Another option would be to redraw the design on the fabric section, using your pattern as a guide, carefully re-creating the measurements.

Use the following shortcut to create a mirror image and ensure a perfect match for the center front of the vest. Mark the garment and pattern lines with wash-out chalk on one front side. Place on a firm surface, right side up, cover with the unmarked piece. Use a rolling pin or brayer to transfer the chalk to the other piece. Markings will be faint, so retrace lightly.

As a design option, consider placing the motifs on the diagonal. You can also use checks instead of the plaid.

Equip your machine with an embroidery needle (90/14) and thread the machine with a 30-weight solid-color embroidery thread. The plaid design lines may not be visually strong enough with variegated thread, yet that may be the look you would like. Experiment! Use a lightweight thread in the bobbin.

To stitch the plaid section, begin and end all lines one inch beyond the marked pattern line. There is no advantage to stitching with a straight stitch first for this design, so set your machine to a narrow, yet slightly open zigzag (about .40 or .50 long and 2.0 or 2.5 wide).

Sew the lines that are under other lines first. For the vest shown on page 80, it is the vertical lines. Your choice of thread color may dictate where to begin. Lighter and brighter colors will be more prominent, so be sure to test the impact of their placement. Repeat with all plaid fabric sections.

Photo 38: Twice As Nice vest (reverse side). Simple computerized machine stitches were used for these designs.

The Wholecloth Garment Stori

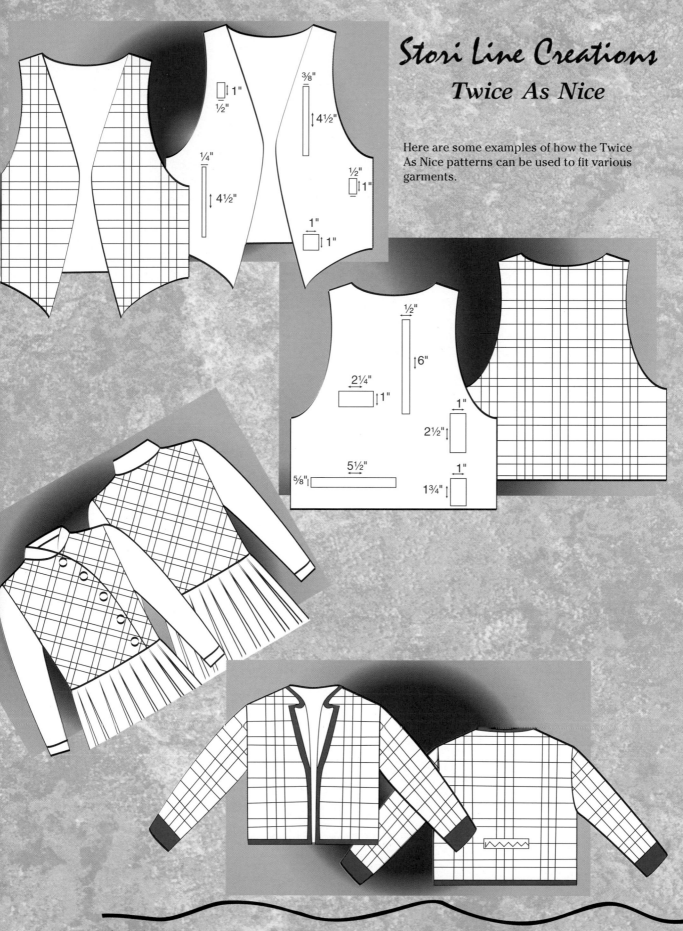

Stori Line Creations
Twice As Nice

Here are some examples of how the Twice As Nice patterns can be used to fit various garments.

1"
½"

3⁄8"

4½"

¼"

4½"

½"
1"

1"
1"

½"
6"

2¼"
1"

1"
2½"

5½"
5⁄8"

1"
1¾"

Photo 39: Twice As Nice vest (plaid side). Planning will ensure that the design lines meet at the front opening.

Photo 40: Twice As Nice vest (reverse side). Visual interest is added with the creation of the madras "windows."

Twice As Nice Stori Lines

Reverse Side

Unless you plan to use more motifs than shown, mark the plain fabric sections with your correct-size pattern pieces.

Measure and mark the location of the fabric windows. See the Stori Line Creations on page 81 for suggested locations and sizes. Your garment style and size may dictate some minor changes.

Create fabric windows as illustrated on page 83.

For a faster approach, or if your machine is not equipped with preprogrammed stitches, consider using just the fabric windows as design elements. You can change their placement and add more, if you like.

Review the embroidery stitches available to you on your machine. The vest features three motifs: stars (approximately ¼" diameter), moons (approximately ⅛" wide x ¾" long), and interconnected squares (¼" wide x 1" to 2" long to symbolize satellites). Any number of small motifs can be substituted. Designs with concentrated stitches will be more visual. Again, test your selections before committing them to the vest.

Stitch the desired programmed designs, scattering them randomly within the boundaries of the vest.

Sew as many of the designs as you like in one color, sprinkling them throughout the vest before switching to another color. Scraps of paper or a tear-away product placed under the fabric will prevent puckering.

Keep these programmed designs about ½" to 1" away from the seam allowance to avoid losing them during construction.

Fabric Windows

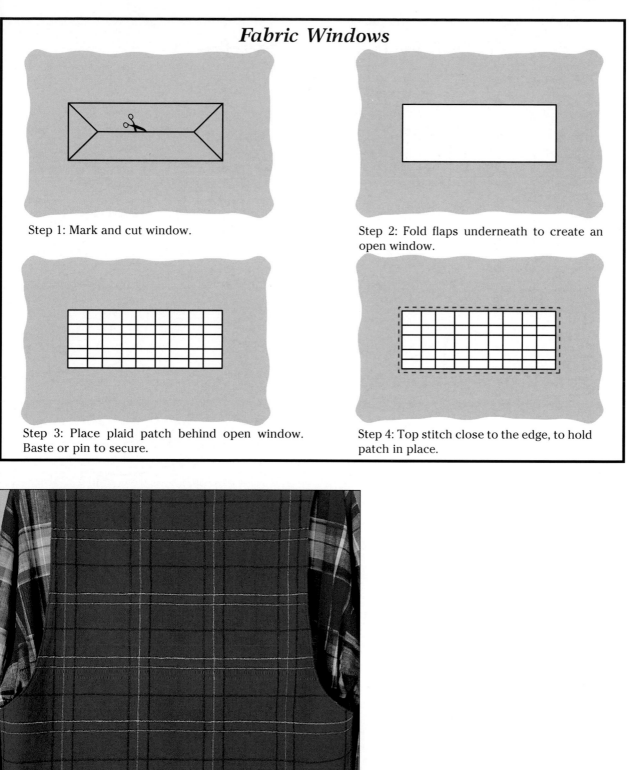

Step 1: Mark and cut window.

Step 2: Fold flaps underneath to create an open window.

Step 3: Place plaid patch behind open window. Baste or pin to secure.

Step 4: Top stitch close to the edge, to hold patch in place.

Photo 41: Twice As Nice vest (plaid back view). "Plaid" fabric was created quickly and easily by stitching with solid colors of 30-weight rayon thread.

Design Elements

Pretty & Pink
Design A

Pretty & Pink
begins on page 27.
See the full-size pattern sheets
for more designs.

Pretty & Pink
Design B

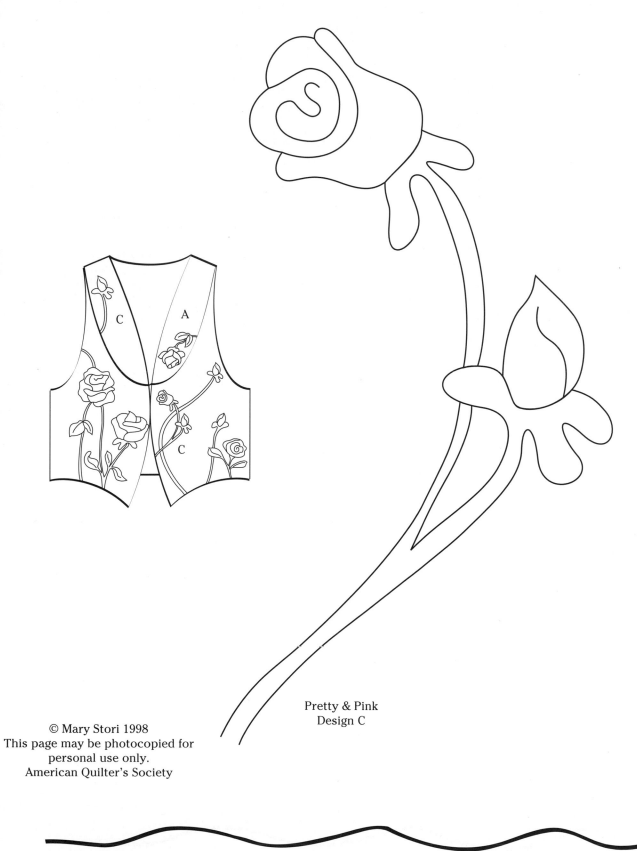

Pretty & Pink
Design C

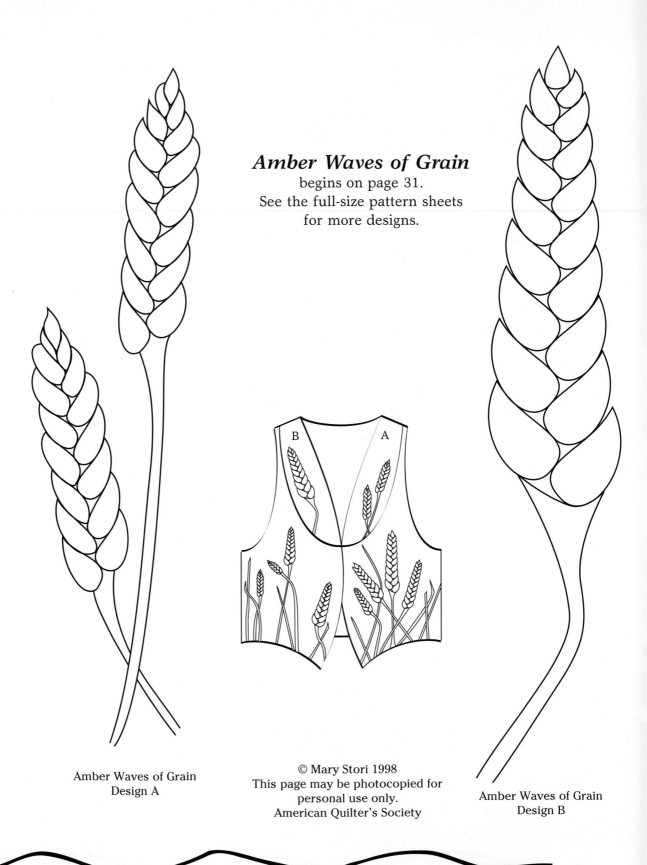

Amber Waves of Grain
begins on page 31.
See the full-size pattern sheets
for more designs.

Amber Waves of Grain
Design A

© Mary Stori 1998
This page may be photocopied for
personal use only.
American Quilter's Society

Amber Waves of Grain
Design B

The Wholecloth Garment Stori

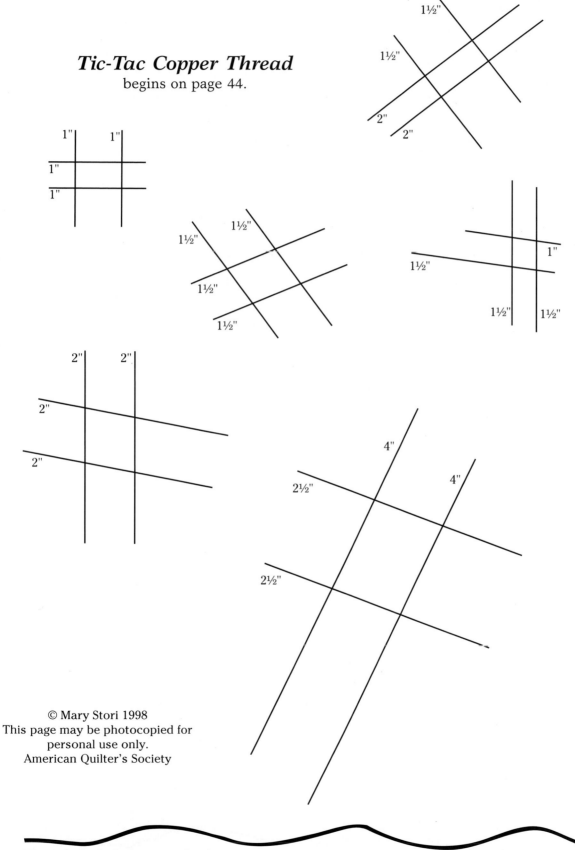

Tic-Tac Copper Thread
begins on page 44.

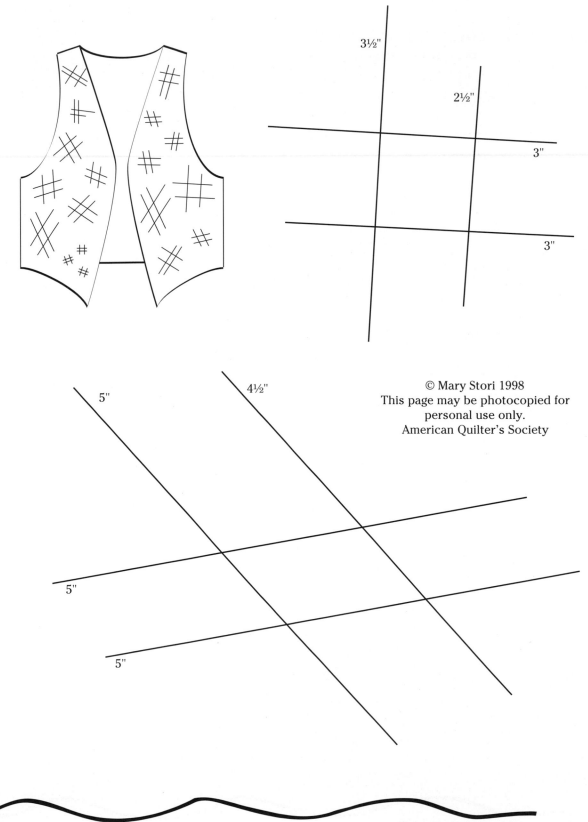

3½"

2½"

3"

3"

5"

4½"

5"

5"

© Mary Stori 1998
This page may be photocopied for
personal use only.
American Quilter's Society

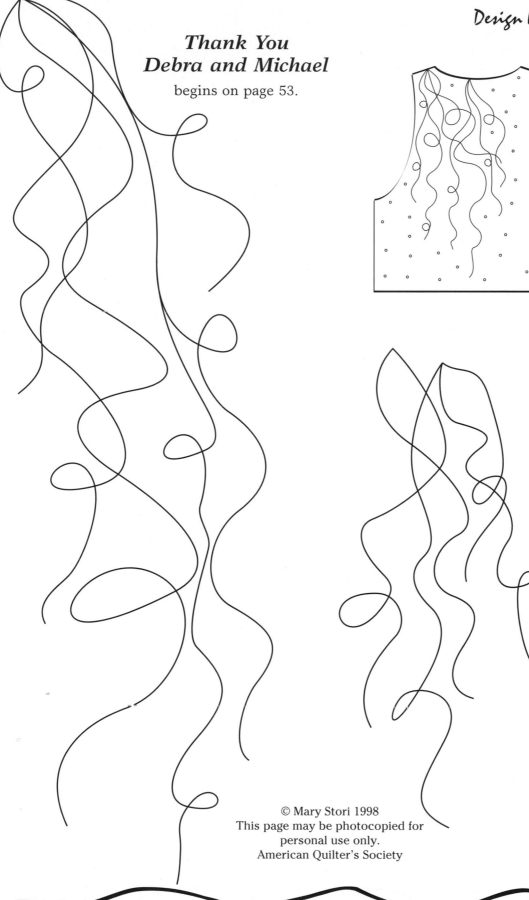

Thank You
Debra and Michael

begins on page 53.

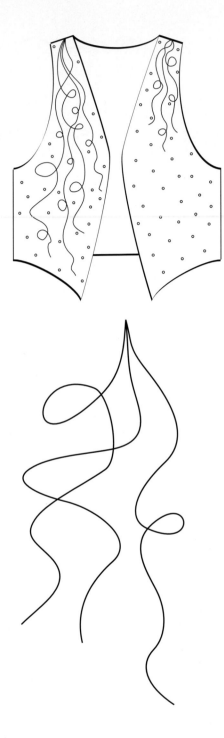

You will want to enlarge these streamers to fit your garment and to make them easier to sew. Or, you can have fun drawing your own squiggles. Just be sure the lines are far enough apart to sew with a zigzag stitch.

Always Wavering
begins on page 58.

Design Elements

Mad for Plaid
begins on page 66.

Heat Lightning
begins on page 70.

Design Elements

© Mary Stori 1998
This page may be photocopied for
personal use only.
American Quilter's Society

The Wholecloth Garment Stori

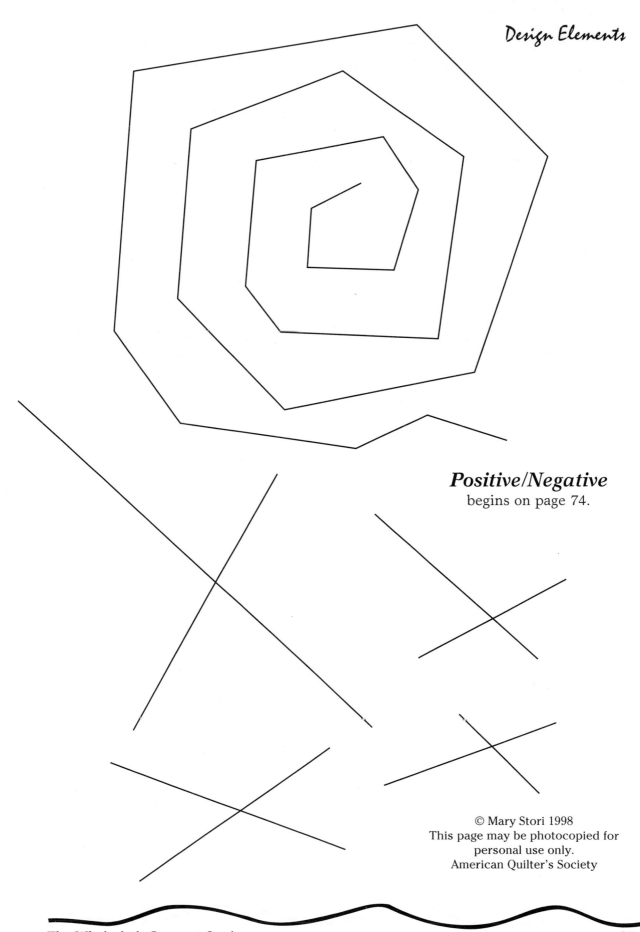

Positive/Negative
begins on page 74.

The Wholecloth Garment Stori

The Wholecloth Garment Stori

Caught in the Web
project begins on page 23.

Indicates lines that extend to edge of garment pattern.

Web
Design A

Stori Lines

Mary Stori gives helpful hints for using her patterns in "Stori Lines" throughout the book. Here are some general suggestions to get you started.

Study the motif layout for your garment. Determine which templates might best fit your garment pieces. Reposition and play with the design as needed.

If the designs don't fit as provided, consider either adding more lines to enlarge them or eliminating some lines to better fit the garment's shape.

Connector lines between the motifs help the designs work together. If the ones shown won't translate to your garment shape, simply draw new ones.

Be sure to extend some of the connector lines to run through any large unquilted areas to hold the batting in place.

Keep important design elements about an inch away from seam allowances to avoid lopping off part of the design when the garment is cut to size.

These full-sized motifs can be traced as given or customized to suit your needs. See "Designing on Paper," page 8, and "Designing on Fabric," page 10, for information on how to use these designer patterns.

Spring Green
Design F

Spring Green
project begins on page 36 .

Web
Design C

The **Wholecloth**
Garment
Stori
©Mary Stori 1998

Pretty & Pink project begins on page 27.

The **Wholecloth**
Garment
Stori
©Mary Stori 1998

Pretty & Pink
Design D

Pretty & Pink
Design F

Pretty & Pink
Design E

*Indicates stem end at jumper armhole. Add a rose bud for other garment styles.

Pretty & Pink
Design A

Pretty & Pink
Design C

Pretty & Pink
Design B

These full-sized motifs can be traced as given or customized to suit your needs. See "Designing on Paper," page 8, and "Designing on Fabric," page 10, for information on how to use these designer patterns.

Special Stories

Mary Stori shares some simple techniques that can give your garments a more professional finish and add that extra special touch. Look for these helpful tips and techniques:

Products & Sources

Batting

Thermore Batting
Hobbs Bonded Fibers
P.O. Box 2521
Waco, TX 76702

Batting and Light Boxes

PineTree Quiltworks, Ltd.
585 Broadway
South Portland, ME 04106
(207) 799-7357; fax (207) 799-9541
Shop phone: (207) 799-9535

Beads and Supplies

TWE/BEADS
P.O. Box 55
Hamburg, NJ 07419-0055
(973) 209-1517
e-mail: info@twebeads.com

Fusible Tricot Interfacing

Ghee's
2620 Centenary Blvd. #2-250
Shreveport, LA 71104
(318) 226-1701
fax: (318) 226-1781
e-mail: ghees@softdisk.com

Nancy's Notions
333 Beichl Avenue
P.O. Box 683
Beaver Dam, WI 53916-0683
(800) 833-0690

Irons and Iron Systems

Euro-Pro
178 W. Service Road
Champlain, NY 12919
(800) 798-7395
Call for location of nearest dealer.

Quilt Frames

Flynn Frame Company
1000 Shiloh Overpass Rd.
Billings, MT 59106
(800) 745-3596

Sewing Machines and Iron Systems

Pfaff American Sales
610 Winters Avenue
P.O. Box 566
Paramus, NJ 07653-0566
(201) 262-7211

Threads and Stabilizers

Web of Thread
1410 Broadway
Paducah, KY 42001
(502) 575-9700
(800) 955-8185—orders only

About the Author

Instead of garnishing food, former cooking instructor Mary Stori now embellishes cloth. As a lecturer, teacher, author, judge, and quilter, Mary's work has appeared frequently in national shows, and she has won many awards. Her garments have traveled with four Fairfield Fashion Shows.

Mary has written numerous articles and has been featured in many quilting magazines. Her first book, *The Stori Book Of Embellishing* (AQS), was published in 1994. She designed The Mary Stori Collection for Kona Bay Fabrics and her own trapunto stencil line for Quilting Creations International, Inc.

"I love the challenge of creating one-of-a-kind fashions and quilts," Mary says. "And traveling throughout the country to present lectures, workshops, and fashion shows keeps me motivated."

AQS Books on Quilts

This is only a partial listing of the books on quilts that are available from the American Quilter's Society. AQS books are known the world [ ] their timely topics, clear writing, beautiful color photographs, and accurate illustrations and patterns. The following books are available from y[ ] bookseller, quilt shop, or public library. If you are unable to locate certain titles in your area, you may order by mail from the AMERICAN QU[ ] SOCIETY, P.O. Box 3290, Paducah, KY 42002-3290. Add $2.00 for postage for the first book ordered and 40¢ for each additional book. Incl[ ] number, title, and price when ordering. Allow 14 to 21 days for delivery. Customers with Visa, MasterCard, or Discover may phone in ord[ ] 7:00–5:00 CST, Monday–Friday, Toll Free 1-800-626-5420.

4595	**Above & Beyond Basics**, Karen Kay Buckley $18.95	4911	**Mariner's Compass Quilts: New Quilts from an Old Favorite** ....
2282	**Adapting Architectural Details for Quilts**, Carol Wagner $12.95	4752	**Miniature Quilts: Connecting New & Old Worlds**, Tina M. Gravatt....
4813	**Addresses & Birthdays**, compiled by Klaudeen Hansen **(HB)**..........$14.95	4514	**Mola Techniques for Today's Quilters**, Charlotte Patera..................
4543	**American Quilt Blocks: 50 Patterns for 50 States**, Beth Summers...........$16.95	3330	**More Projects and Patterns**, Judy Florence...........................
4696	**Amish Kinder Komforts**, Bettina Havig..........................$14.95	1981	**Nancy Crow: Quilts and Influences**, Nancy Crow.................
4829	**Anita Shackelford: Surface Textures**, Anita Shackelford **(HB)** $24.95	3331	**Nancy Crow: Work in Transition**, Nancy Crow ....
4899	**Appliqué Paper Greetings**, Elly Sienkiewicz **(HB)**.......................$24.95	4828	**Nature, Design & Silk Ribbons**, Cathy Grafton...................
3790	**Appliqué Patterns from Native American Beadwork Designs**, Dr. Joyce Mori.................$14.95	3332	**New Jersey Quilts**,The Heritage Quilt Project of New Jersey..............
		3927	**New Patterns from Old Architecture**, Carol Wagner......................
2099	**Ask Helen: More About Quilting Designs**, Helen Squire $14.95	2153	**No Dragons on My Quilt**, Jean Ray Laury..........................
2207	**Award-Winning Quilts: 1985-1987** $24.95	4627	**Ohio Star Quilts: New Quilts from an Old Favorite** ....
2354	**Award-Winning Quilts: 1988-1989** $24.95	3469	**Old Favorites in Miniature**, Tina Gravatt........................
3425	**Award-Winning Quilts: 1990-1991** $24.95	4831`	**Optical Illusions for Quilters**, Karen Combs.....................
3791	**Award-Winning Quilts: 1992-1993** $24.95	4515	**Paint and Patches: Painting on Fabrics with Pigment**, Vicki L. Johns
4830	**Baskets: Celtic Style**, Scarlett Rose............................$19.95	5098	**Pineapple Quilts, New Quilts from an Old Favorite** ....
4832	**A Batch of Patchwork**, May T. Miller & Susan B. Burton $18.95	4513	**Plaited Patchwork**, Shari Cole ....
4593	**Blossoms by the Sea: Making Ribbon Flowers for Quilts**, Faye Labanaris $24.95	3928	**Precision Patchwork for Scrap Quilts**, Jeannette Tousley Muir ....
4898	**Borders & Finishing Touches**, Bonnie K. Browning $16.95	4779	**Protecting Your Quilts: A Guide for Quilt Owners, Second Edition** ....
4697	**Caryl Bryer Fallert: A Spectrum of Quilts, 1983-1995**, Caryl Bryer Fallert $24.95	4542	**A Quilted Christmas**, edited by Bonnie Browning...................
4626	**Celtic Geometric Quilts**, Camille Remme $16.95	2380	**Quilter's Registry**, Lynne Fritz ....
3926	**Celtic Style Floral Appliqué**, Scarlett Rose.........$14.95	3467	**Quilting Patterns from Native American Designs**, Dr. Joyce Mori ......
2208	**Classic Basket Quilts**, Elizabeth Porter & Marianne Fons.........$16.95	3470	**Quilting with Style**, Gwen Marston & Joe Cunningham ....
2355	**Creative Machine Art**, Sharee Dawn Roberts $24.95	2284	**Quiltmaker's Guide: Basics & Beyond**, Carol Doak..................
4818	**Dear Helen, Can You Tell Me?** Helen Squire $15.95	4918	**Quilts by Paul D. Pilgrim: Blending the Old & the New**, Gerald E. Roy......
3399	**Dye Painting!** Ann Johnston.........$19.95	2257	*Quilts:* **The Permanent Collection – MAQS** ....
4814	**Encyclopedia of Designs for Quilting**, Phyllis D. Miller **(HB)** $34.95	3793	*Quilts:* **The Permanent Collection – MAQS Volume II** ....
3468	**Encyclopedia of Pieced Quilt Patterns**, compiled by Barbara Brackman ...$34.95	3789	**Roots, Feathers & Blooms**, Linda Giesler Carlson..................
3846	**Fabric Postcards**, Judi Warren.........$22.95	4512	**Sampler Quilt Blocks from Native American Designs**, Dr. Joyce Mor
4594	**Firm Foundations**, Jane Hall & Dixie Haywood.........$18.95	3796	**Seasons of the Heart & Home: Quilts for a Winter's Day**, Jan Patek
4900	**Four Blocks Continued...**, Linda Giesler Carlson.........$16.95	3761	**Seasons of the Heart & Home: Quilts for Summer Days**, Jan Patek
2381	**From Basics to Binding**, Karen Kay Buckley.........$16.95	2357	**Sensational Scrap Quilts**, Darra Duffy Williamson...............
4526	**Gatherings: America's Quilt Heritage**, Kathlyn F. Sullivan.........$34.95	4783	**Silk Ribbons by Machine**, Jeanie Sexton......................
2097	**Heirloom Miniatures**, Tina M. Gravatt.........$9.95	3929	**The Stori Book of Embellishing**, Mary Stori.....................
4628	**Helen's Guide to quilting in the 21st century**, Helen Squire.........$16.95	3903	**Straight Stitch Machine Appliqué**, Letty Martin..................
1906	**Irish Chain Quilts: A Workbook of Irish Chains**, Joyce B. Peaden $14.95	3792	**Striplate Piecing**, Debra Wagner ....
3784	**Jacobean Appliqué: Book I, "Exotica,"** Campbell & Ayars $18.95	5012	**Take-Away Appliqué**, Suzanne Marshall....................
4544	**Jacobean Appliqué: Book II, "Romantica,"** Campbell & Ayars.........$18.95	3930	**Tessellations & Variations**, Barbara Ann Caron...............
3904	**The Judge's Task**, Patricia J. Morris.........$19.95	3788	**Three-Dimensional Appliqué**, Anita Shackelford...............
4751	**Liberated Quiltmaking**, Gwen Marston **(HB)** $24.95	4596	**Ties, Ties, Ties: Traditional Quilts from Neckties**, Janet B. Elwin......
4897	**Lois Smith's Machine Quiltmaking**, Lois Smith.........$19.95	3931	**Time-Span Quilts: New Quilts from Old Tops**, Becky Herdle ....
4523	**Log Cabin Quilts: New Quilts from an Old Favorite** $14.95	4919	**Transforming Fabric**, Carolyn Dahl......................
4545	**Log Cabin with a Twist**, Barbara T. Kaempfer $18.95	2029	**A Treasury of Quilting Designs**, Linda Goodmon Emery............
4815	*Love to Quilt:* **Bears, Bears, Bears**, Karen Kay Buckley.........$14.95	3847	**Tricks with Chintz**, Nancy S. Breland ....
4833	*Love to Quilt:* **Broderie Perse: The Elegant Quilt**, Barbara W. Barber $14.95	5014	**The Wholecloth Garment Stori**, Mary Stori...................
4890	*Love to Quilt:* **Dye & Discharge**, Sara Newberg King $14.95	2286	**Wonderful Wearables: A Celebration of Creative Clothing**, Virginia Avery
4598	*Love to Quilt:* **Men's Vests**, Alexandra Capadalis Dupré.........$14.95	4812	**Who's Who in American Quilting**, edited by Bonnie Browning **(HB)**....
4816	*Love to Quilt:* **Necktie Sampler Blocks**, Janet B. Elwin $14.95	4956	**Variegreat! New Dimensions in Traditional Quilts**, Linda Glantz ...
4753	*Love to Quilt:* **Penny Squares**, Willa Baranowski $12.95	4972	**20th Century Quilts**, Cuesta Benberry and Joyce Gross ....
4995	**Magic Stack-n-Whack Quilts**, Bethany S. Reynolds $19.95		